THE BRIGHTON BARD

WINS, GRINS & LIMBS

A POETIC REVIEW OF **BRIGHTON & HOVE ALBION'S** HISTORIC 22/23 SEASON

Cover image by: Margarita Dimova
Book design by: SWATT Books Ltd

Printed in the United Kingdom
First Printing, 2023

ISBN: 978-1-7395701-0-1 (Paperback)

The Brighton Bard
Brighton, Sussex
@TheBrightonBard

THANK YOUS

Firstly, I'd like to thank Paul Hazlewood, Brighton and Hove Albion Senior Club Photographer, for his help and advice with this project. Once I'd had the initial idea for the book, I wasn't sure what the next step should be, but, having published several himself, his insights into the process has made the journey so much easier. I am very, very grateful.

Separately, I'd like to thank Paul and Brighton and Hove Albion for permitting me to use some of the images Paul captured in this most special of seasons. This stunning visual element has added so much to the book and brings the words to life in a way nothing else could.

Finally, I'd like to thank Sam Pearce at SWATT Books (swatt-books.co.uk) for her help in the design and publishing process and to Maunie Catcheside from Brighton & Hove PR for organising the press relations in the build-up to the book's launch.

CONTENTS

INTRODUCTION

I can remember the moment clearly.

It was 9 pm on Monday, 12 August 2019, and I was lying in bed chatting to my wife about our new life together in the U.S.A. We'd only been married for a few weeks, but I'd known for months that living in America would mean I'd miss many aspects of Brighton & Hove – a place I'd called home for over 30 years.

And one of the biggest things I'd miss would be supporting the Albion.

I'd never been a big user of social media, had never logged onto a fan forum, and didn't even have an account on the likes of Twitter or Instagram, but as I lay there, an idea formed. Maybe social media could be a way of staying connected with the club and community back in Sussex. And why not use rhymes as content? After all, I'd been writing humorous ones in birthday cards for friends and family for years.

I jumped out of bed and grabbed my phone.

The username was available!

@TheBrightonBard was born.

As I type, it is almost four years since that night, and I hope the hundreds of lighthearted poems I've shared since have helped raise a smile here and there for fellow Albion fans. In a world where social media can be so divisive, I've tried to use the account as a force for good (despite the best efforts of Palace, Chelsea and VAR!) and count myself very lucky to still feel so connected to our club, city and county whilst living 4500 miles away. The connection has made moving overseas so much easier.

Which brings me to the book you're holding right now.

Although the idea of using rhymes to create a 22/23 review came to me mid-season, work commitments meant I couldn't get started until late March '23, and it has taken over my life in a way I didn't anticipate! It's taken me hundreds of hours to create as, whilst I was able to base most of the pre/post-match rhymes on poems I'd already shared on social media, 90% of the 650+ in-match rhymes are new, which meant I had to review every game on Albion T.V. or via YouTube.

As you can imagine, it was a painstakingly slow process that involved pausing each game multiple times in order to write a rhyme for each notable incident.

But I hope you feel it was worth it.

The games are presented chronologically with match stats and a (non-rhyming) preview, followed by one pre-match rhyme, 15 in-match rhymes, and one post-match rhyme. My written content is accompanied by stunning match-day images from Brighton and Hove Albion Senior Club Photographer, Paul Hazlewood. Paul has been such a support, and I'd like to express my immense gratitude to him and the club for allowing me to use them.

Finally, I'm very proud to be supporting the BHAFC Foundation. For over 30 years, the club's official charity has been using the power of football to engage and inspire people to make good life choices and help reduce inequalities in Sussex, and £5 from the sale of each book will go directly to the Foundation to help ensure that this important work continues.

I hope you enjoy reliving our historic 22/23 season.

Cheers everyone, and up the Albion!

The Brighton Bard
August 2023
TheBrightonBard.com
@thebrightonbard on social media

SUPPORTING THE COMMUNITY

FOUNDATION

The Brighton & Hove Albion Foundation — the official charity of the Albion — use the power of football to change lives across Sussex every single day.

As you are probably aware, while you once knew us as Albion in the Community, our name has now changed. Our work will remain as community-focused as ever, and this name change brings us even closer to the football club.

Reaching more than 5,000 people every week, and around 20,000 people a year, the Foundation brings the Albion badge directly into local communities in 35 towns and cities across Sussex.

Our work focuses on three main areas: getting people active and playing football, helping people learn new skills and improve their employability, and improving the health and wellbeing of local communities.

Most of our programmes are aimed at children, young people living in communities where there is greatest need, or people with a disability; making football a sport for everyone, championing equality, and supporting people to overcome any barriers to taking part.

As C.E.O., I'm lucky enough to have met countless amazing people during my time with the Foundation. I've met children with a challenging homelife who have blossomed into happy and successful adults, some of whom have even gone on to work with us at the Foundation. I've met men going through dark times, who find connection and friendship at our men's mental health football sessions. I've met people with a wide range of disabilities, from amputees, people with Downs syndrome and people with a vision impairment, who have all struggled to enjoy the beautiful game until they found our disability football programme. The one thing that ties them all together: The power of football that connects us and provides a place where we belong and can be accepted.

We provide access to football for thousands of kids, we champion girls participation in the sport through our female pathway, we run one of the biggest disability football programmes in England, we mentor young people to help them make good life choices, we work with more than 160 schools supporting children's education, and so much more in between.

Our work really is a group effort; a concerted attempt from so many organisations to use football's massive appeal to change lives. Between the Foundation, the Albion, the Premier League, our title partners American Express, schools, local government, the police, the N.H.S., and many more groups, we're all working together to help our local communities thrive.

Find out more at: bhafcfoundation.org.uk

We're delighted that, through the purchase of Wins, Grins & Limbs, you'll be directly supporting the work that we do,

Up the Albion!

Matt Dorn
Chief Executive
Brighton & Hove Albion Foundation

MATCH #1

Sunday, 7 August 2022

Manchester United 1 – 2 Brighton & Hove Albion

Competition: **Premier League**
Kick-off: **14:00**
Venue: **Old Trafford, Manchester**
Weather: **21c, sunny**
Referee: **Paul Tierney**
Attendance: **73,711**

Squads

Manchester United: de Gea, Dalot, Maguire, Li Martínez, Shaw (Malaciaat 90), McTominay (van de Beek 78), Fred (Ronaldo 53), Bruno Fernandes (Garnachoat 90), Sancho (Elanga 90), Eriksen, Rashford. **Unused subs:** Varane, Heaton, Wan-Bissaka, Garner.

Albion: Sanchez, Veltman, Dunk, Webster, March (Colwill 90), Caicedo, Lallana (Mwepu 75), Gross, Trossard (Lamptey 75), Welbeck (Undav 90+1). **Unused subs:** Steele, Maupay, Sarmiento, Mitoma, van Hecke.

Match Preview

As opening games of the season go, they don't get much more challenging than away at Manchester United.

Following pre-season training in Portugal, we headed to Old Trafford fresh from a promising 5-1 win in a friendly over Espanyol at the Amex the previous weekend.

Leandro Trossard had taken the plaudits against the La Liga team after netting a hat-trick, and our Belgian winger would be hoping to maintain his goalscoring form against a team against whom we'd enjoyed one of our best Premier League wins over a few months earlier. In that game, Trossard had rounded off the scoring in a 4-0 rout of United at the Amex, but a lot had changed for the hosts since that encounter.

After a somewhat disappointing reign, interim boss Ralf Rangnick had left Old Trafford, and the United board had turned to Ajax's Erik ten Hag to replace him. In turn, ten Hag had bolstered his ranks with some impressive signings, including Christian Eriksen.

The opening game marked the start of Graham Potter's fourth season as our head coach, and aside from long-term absentee Jakub Moder, he reported no additional injuries.

It was a beautiful, sunny August afternoon in Manchester as we looked to repeat the heroics from late last season.

And what an afternoon it was.

5
14
WELBECK
18
LALLANA
14
13
MAGUIRE
5
13

Pre-Match Ryhme

United have Eriksen & Ronaldo,
But us seagulls, we aren't scared,
As last time at the Amex,
They looked a little ill-prepared.

The day is bright, the sun is out,
The temperature reads 21.
Here we go, a new season starts,
This one could be fun.

In-Match Rhymes

1m: KICK-OFF

Expectations are high,
It's a beautiful day.
We beat them at home,
Now let's beat them away.

↓

1m: EARLY CHANCE FOR LEO!!

The early pace,
We are setting.
Leandro shoots,
Oh, side-netting!

↓

27m: LUCKY LAD.

McTominay leaves Moises,
Writhing on the floor.
He's shown a yellow,
Could have been more.

↓

30m: ALBION TAKE THE LEAD!!! (0-1)

It's a super cross from Danny,
On a six-pence put.
It's a tap-in for Gross,
WITH HIS TRUSTY RIGHT FOOT!!!

↓

32m: A PENNY FOR HIS THOUGHTS

I wonder if United,
Ronaldo will soon ditch.
As he's sitting on the bench
Thinking, "why aren't I on the pitch"?

37m: WELBECK VOLLEYS WIDE

From Lallana's cross,
Danny beats Maguire.
Bloody hell,
We're on fire!

↓

39m: GROSS DOUBLES OUR LEAD!!! (0-2)

Oh, Pascal,
His touch was deft!
And this time it was with,
HIS TRUSTY LEFT!!!!

↓

HALF-TIME RHYME

Hey, United,
What's the score?
As we're predicting,
Another nil to four!

↓

53m: MAGUIRE WRESTLES TROSSARD,

It's like the WWE,
Seems unwise.
Hey, Harry, pick on someone,
Your own size!

↓

53m: UNITED SUBSTITUTION

Ronaldo's on,
So it won't be long,
Until the ref,
He'll try to con.

67m: SANCHEZ DENIES ERIKSEN

Right-foot strike,
Eriksen lets go.
Superb right-hand save,
Struck hard and low.

↓

68m: UNITED PULL ONE BACK (1-2)

A United corner,
Rob could have been bolder.
An Alexis own goal,
After hitting Dalot's shoulder.

↓

73m: MOMENTUM WITH UNITED

Dalot shoots,
Low and hard it's drilled.
Lallana clears,
After Sanchez spills.

↓

76m: ALBION HOLDING ON

Equaliser briefly,
On the cards.
As Martinez shoots over,
From 25 yards.

↓

90+6m: FINAL WHISTLE

"Albion, Albion",
We sing our song.
It's all over,
AND WE HUNG ON!!!! (WOW!!)

Post-Match Ryhme

In seasons past, I have to say,
That would have been a draw.
We go ahead, then lose our nerve,
And then they bloody score.

But not this season; what a win!
In the Premier League, things are changing.
As the 'top six' have become a bit complacent,
And things need rearranging!

MATCH #2

Saturday, 13 August 2022

Brighton & Hove Albion 0 – 0 Newcastle United

Competition: **Premier League**
Kick-off: **15:00**
Venue: **The Amex Stadium, Brighton**
Weather: **29c, sunny**
Referee: **Graham Scott**
Attendance: **31,552**

Squad

Albion: Sanchez, Veltman, Dunk, Webster, Trossard (Mitoma 75), Mac Allister, Caicedo, Trossard, Gross, Lallana (Mwepu 65), March (Lamptey 75), Welbeck. **Unused subs:** Steele, Colwill, Alzate, Sarmiento, Undav, van Hecke.

Newcastle United: Pope, Trippier, Schär, Botman, Burn, Willock (S Longstaff 76), Bruno Guimarães, Joelinton, Almirón, Wilson (Wood 87), Saint-Maximin (Murphy 75). **Unused subs:** Dúbravka, Dummett, Lascelles, Ritchie, Manquillo, Anderson.

Match Preview

Whilst many prefer to have the first game of the season at home, the fact we were coming off an impressive away win at Old Trafford arguably heightened the pre-match anticipation and gave us a real chance to build on the stunning victory from six days earlier.

Following the heroics in Manchester, including the 2021/22 campaign, we had lost only one of our last ten Premier League outings (a 3-0 defeat at Manchester City) and were unbeaten at home in our previous three matches.

Newcastle had enjoyed an opening day victory of their own the previous weekend with a 2-0 defeat over newly promoted and Premier League debutants Nottingham Forest.

The game had marked the start of the first full season under the ownership of the Saudi Arabia Public Investment Fund, which had taken over the Magpies 10 months earlier. Manager Eddie Howe had been busy spending the new owners' money over the summer, including signing Matt Targett on a permanent deal from Aston Villa. At the same time, Nick Pope had arrived from relegated Burnley.

With Graham Potter announcing we had no new injury concerns, it was a traditional Saturday afternoon kick-off at a sweltering Amex as we looked to make it back-to-back Premier League wins whilst taking on a club that was now, on paper, one of the richest in the world.

14
11
MAXIMIN
10
7

Pre-Match Ryhme

It's our first home game of the season,
And we welcome the Geordies here.
It's impressive they've sold out their allocation,
As Newcastle ain't that near.

Passionate fans, decent folk,
And often very funny.
After years without, they're dreaming of success,
As suddenly, they've loads of money.

In-Match Rhymes

1m: KICK-OFF

It's a scorching Saturday,
Three o'clock.
If you're in the east stand,
You're going to need sunblock.

↓

13m: REALLY?

It happens so often,
It could be a meme.
Almirón buys a foul,
And then finds the need to scream.

↓

20m: TROSSARD DENIED

A super break by Leo,
On the left wing.
He crosses for Danny,
But to the ball, Pope clings.

↓

22m: EASY

A lofted free kick,
Newcastle try.
Bread and butter for Sanchez,
Who can leap 15ft high.

↓

22m: YOU AIN'T FOOLING ANYBODY

At the edge of our area,
A slight altercation.
Saint-Maximin goes down,
Booked for (poor) simulation.

30m: PENALTY?

We claim handball,
But the ref replied,
That the defender's arm,
Was by his side.

↓

37m: 30-YARD EFFORT SAVED

Decent break,
The crowd shout 'shoot'.
Moises let's one fly,
With his right boot.

↓

HALF-TIME RHYME

Pretty even,
At half-time.
Away support singing,
Fog on the Tyne.

↓

49m: LALLANA DENIED

Solly's cross,
Adam gives a shout.
It's a free header,
But Pope claws it out.

↓

57m: CALM DOWN!

Solly and Joelinton,
Daggers drawn.
Both teams wade in,
Handbags at dawn.

75m: ALBION SUBSTITUTION

Solly off,
Lamptey on.
Who's even faster,
And just as strong.

↓

75m: KAORU'S DEBUT

Now Trossard's replaced,
By Mitoma.
I can spot this guy's good,
From Oklahoma!

↓

82m: CLEARED OFF THE LINE!!

Veltman shoots,
With bated breath we wait.
The ref looks at his watch,
But it does not vibrate.

↓

85m: OH, PASCAL!

Mitoma is a thorn,
In Newcastle's side.
He sets one up for Gross,
Who fires just wide.

↓

90+5m: FINAL WHISTLE

Down the barrel,
Of defeat, they stared.
But Newcastle hang on,
The points are shared.

Post-Match Ryhme

I'm a little bit frustrated,
And must be honest and say,
As, in my view, despite loads of chances,
Things just did not go our way.

We pushed forward with real purpose,
But it seemed time after bloomin' time,
Our efforts flew wide, their keeper saved,
Or a defender managed to clear it off the line.

MATCH #3

Sunday, 21 August 2022

West Ham United 0 – 2 Brighton & Hove Albion

Competition: **Premier League**
Kick-off: **14:00**
Venue: **The London Stadium, London**
Weather: **24c, sunny**
Referee: **Anthony Taylor**
Attendance: **62,449**

Squads

West Ham: Fabianski, Coufal (Johnson 75), Zouma, Kehrer, Cresswell, Soucek, Rice, Bowen, Fornals (Scamacca 62), Benrahma (Lanzini 75), Antonio (Cornet 74). **Unused subs**: Downes, Areola, Ogbonna, Coventry, Ashby.

Albion: Sanchez, Veltman, Dunk, Webster, March (Mwepu 85), Lallana (Estupinan 62), Caciedo, Mac Allister, Trossard (Mitoma 90+2), Gross, Welbeck. **Unused subs:** Steele, Lamptey, Colwill, Maupay, Alzate, Undav.

Match Preview

Hopes were high as we headed to the London Stadium as we looked to maintain our unbeaten start to the season. We were yet to lose a Premier League meeting with the Hammers, winning four and drawing six of our ten encounters. We had also scored in all ten games, although we'd only kept clean sheets in two of them and none in the last seven.

Meanwhile, despite finishing seventh last season and qualifying for the Europa Conference League, David Moyes' side had got off to a disappointing start with losses at home to champions Manchester City on the opening day before losing 1-0 at new boys Nottingham Forest at the city ground the previous week.

In his pre-match press conference, Graham Potter revealed no fresh injury worries (only Jakub Moder was absent as he continued his rehab following knee surgery), confirming that new signing Pervis Estupinan would be in the squad.

Our head coach expressed his excitement about the new signing, commenting, "Pervis is an attacking full-back, the club and I have been aware of him. He's got some attributes that we think will help us. He needs time to settle in, but we've been impressed so far. He will be in the squad for Sunday's game."

He got on, and he was brilliant!

betw
30
AMERICAN EXPRESS
10
5
22
DUNK
5
13
betway

MARCH
7
STACK
UD

Pre-Match Ryhme

We're heading up to East London,
Where the Olympics were once held.
I, for one, am confident,
That West Ham can be felled.

We've started the season strongly,
Claiming four points out of six.
Who else out there is with me?
An away win, I predicts!

In-Match Rhymes

1m: KICK-OFF

Home fans sing,
Decent sound,
As bubbles float,
Around the ground.

↓

2m: EARLY CHANCE FOR WEST HAM

Fizzing right-foot shot,
From Benrahma.
Flies past the post,
Early drama.

↓

19m: PENALTY TO US!

Break by Trossard,
Ball to Danny, when,
His heel gets clipped,
Certain pen!

↓

22m: NO ONE BETTER

VAR confirms,
Pen? Dead cert.
Up steps Alexis,
To convert.

↓

22m: GOAL!!!!!! (0-1)

Waits for eight seconds,
Before he takes the kick.
Oh, Mac Allister,
That'll do the trick!

26m: ALBION PRESSURE

We've just had two corners,
In succession.
Ahead in goals,
And possession.

↓

HALF-TIME RHYME

Halfway there,
Great display.
Can we make it two from three,
Both played away?

↓

50m: CLASSY

We're in control,
Dominating possession.
It sometimes feels like watching,
A training session.

↓

62m: ALBION SUBSTITUTION

Here he comes,
He's the man.
Our new signing,
Pervis Estupinan.

↓

66m: GOAL!!!!! (0-2)

What a move!
Alexis to Gross.
Finished by Leo,
Grandiose!

67m: WHAT A GOAL THAT IS!

You won't see a better,
Goal all season.
But we are Albion,
So it stands to reason.

↓

75m: SOLLY SHOULD HAVE SCORED!

Oh, Solly,
I think we'll win, despite.
But your powerful header,
Should have put us out of sight.

↓

83m: GREAT TIP-OVER BY ROB

Sanchez hasn't,
Had much to do.
Tips a header over,
Across his goal, he flew.

↓

84m: AND AGAIN!

He does the same again,
A minute later.
This time the ball,
Is a little straighter.

↓

90+4m: FINAL WHISTLE

JUST FANTASTIC!!
THE BOYS DELIVER!!
("Oh, not again",
Groans my liver!!)

Post-Match Ryhme

We played magnificently in London,
Great to see us performing well away.
And also great to see our new signing,
Pervis Estupinan play.

Straight away, he seemed to fit right in,
A complete natural at left-back.
Such power and speed, and so good on the break,
Helping us turn defence into attack.

MATCH #4

Wednesday, 24 August 2022

Forest Green Rovers 0 – 3 Brighton & Hove Albion

Competition: **Carabao Cup - second round south**
Kick-off: **19.45**
Venue: **The Bolt New Lawn, Nailsworth**
Weather: **20c, overcast**
Referee: **Tim Robinson**
Attendance: **3,812**

Squads

Forest Green Rovers: McGee, Bernard, Casey, Cargill, Robertson (McAllister 45), Stevenson, Hendry (Davis 62), Little (Peart-Harris 45), O'Keeffe, March (Brown 62), Wickham (Matt 45). **Unused subs:** Matt, Jones, McAllister, Thomas, Peart-Harris, Davis, Bunker, Brown, Bennett.

Albion: Steele, Lamptey (Hinchy 79), Colwill, van Hecke, Turns, Mitoma (Moran 67), Alzate, Spong (Furlong 84), Enciso (Peupion 79), Undav (Offiah 67), Ferguson. **Unused subs:** McGill, Tsoungui.

Match Preview

The second round of the EFL Cup saw us drawn against Forest Green Rovers of League One for only the second time, and with Graham Potter indicating that there would be changes to the squad, we were expecting a very different line-up to that which had beaten West Ham at the London Stadium three days earlier.

Forest Green had experienced an unsettled summer. Having won promotion to League One for the first time in their history the previous season, they lost the manager who had guided them there when Rob Edwards joined Watford.

Edwards was replaced by Ian Burchnall, who had succeeded Graham Potter when our head coach left Swedish club Ostersunds to return to the UK. Burchnall returned in 2020 and was appointed manager of Notts County. Having guided them to the National League playoffs, he had joined Forest Green at the end of the previous season.

With this in mind, their haul of four points from four games was not bad, although this included defeats in their opening two home games. They had reached the second round of the Carabao Cup by beating Leyton Orient 2-0 at The Bolt New Lawn and were hoping to repeat the result on this mild but overcast night under the floodlights.

It was the perfect night to give some squad players some game time.

And they didn't let us down.

22
LAMPTEY
2
20

ecotricity
AMERICAN EXPRESS
21
28
AMERICAN EXPRESS
28
47

Pre-Match Ryhme

We're heading up to Gloucestershire,
11 changes have been made.
The perfect chance to give a run-out,
To some lads who haven't played.

You cannot beat an August evening,
Underneath the lights.
Here we go, time to earn their dough,
Come on, you blue and whites.

In-Match Rhymes

1m: KICK-OFF

A compact ground,
And while we aim to win,
These early-round games,
Can be a banana skin.

↓

3m: LIVELY

Mitoma breaks,
Undav ahead.
Tries to find Enciso,
Blocked instead.

↓

6m: ENCISO FIRES WIDE

Julio Enciso,
Past defenders, ghosts.
Right-foot shot,
Flies past the post.

↓

27m: WOODWORK!

In-swinging corner,
Undav also hits the post.
Debut goal?
Well, almost.

↓

35m: THE HOSTS GO CLOSE

Forest Green's O'Keeffe,
Grazes the bar.
Nice right-foot shot,
Close, but no cigar.

37m: SHOWING MY AGE

Levi Colwill,
The guy's legit.
For our team,
He's a perfect fit. (I'll get my coat)

↓

38m: UNDAV'S FIRST ALBION GOAL!! (0-1)

From Evan Ferguson,
A lovely flick.
Denis, with his left-foot,
That boy is quick!!

↓

45+1m GOOAAALLLLLL!!!! (0-2)

Enciso assist,
Steven Alzate aces.
That's how you strike them,
RIGHT ON THE LACES!!

↓

HALF-TIME RHYME

Two ahead,
Looking good,
It could be more,
Perhaps it should.

↓

54m: JASON STEELE M'LORD

Great save from Steele!
Not an easy height.
McAllister assisted March,
And that does not sound right!

64m: GREAT BREAK

From defence,
We broke fast.
Evan Ferguson,
What a pass.

↓

64m: SHOULD BE THREE!

Cross-field to Undav,
Rises high.
Heads just wide,
Decent try.

↓

73m: ALBION AT FULL-STRETCH

Mayhem in our box,
Think pinball machine.
Luckily they can't finish,
Steele's sheet stays clean.

↓

90+4m: GOAL! (0-3)

A goal for Evan!
Grabs one late.
Finished well,
By number 28.

↓

90+5m: FINAL WHISTLE

Never easy,
But I think the lads had fun.
Squad rotation,
And it's a job well done.

Post-Match Ryhme

Potter made 11 changes,
Many new players were put on stage.
How they'd do in a Premier League game,
Well, that's really hard to gauge.

Anyway, everyone did a perfect job,
And in case you've not received the text,
The draw's been made for the next round,
And it's away at Charlton next.

MATCH #5

Saturday, 27 August 2022

Brighton & Hove Albion 1 – 0 Leeds United

Competition: **Premier League**
Kick-off: **15.00**
Venue: **The Amex Stadium, Brighton**
Weather: **23c, bright**
Referee: **Michael Salisbury**
Attendance: **30,953**

Squads

Albion: Sanchez, Veltman (Lamptey 70), Webster, Dunk, Estupinan (Mitoma 78), March (Mwepu 70), Caicedo, Mac Allister, Trossard (Colwill 78), Gross, Welbeck (van Hecke 88). **Unused subs:** Steele, Alzate, Undav, Ferguson.

Leeds United: Meslier, Kristensen, Koch, Llorente, Struijk, Adams, Roca (Klich 59), James (Sinisterra 59), Aaronson (Gelhardt 82'), Harrison (Forshaw 74), Rodrigo. **Unused subs:** Summerville, Klaesson, Hjelde, Drameh, Greenwood.

Match Preview

It was fifth v third for our fourth Premier League match of the season, and, based on recent results, there was every reason to be optimistic heading into the game.

Albion had an unbeaten record against Leeds in the four matches we'd played since they'd returned to the top-flight in 2020. Having won both games that season, 2-0 at home and 1-0 at Elland Road, both of last season's encounters had ended in draws, 0-0 at the Amex and 1-1 in West Yorkshire in May with Danny Welbeck on the score sheet.

As far as this season was concerned, both teams had identical records after three games — two wins and a draw. Jesse Marsch's side's victories had come at home, 2-1 against Wolves and 3-0 the previous Sunday versus Chelsea, whilst in their only away match, they had been held 2-2 at Southampton.

If we were to avoid defeat, we'd stretch our unbeaten run to nine games going back to the end of the previous season and establish a new top-flight club record.

Graham Potter had named the same team for all three games so far but had been keen to praise the contribution of all the substitutes involved.

With Jeremy Sarmiento the only addition to the injury list (Jakub Moder was still in long-term rehabilitation), it was a 3 pm kick-off on a sultry afternoon at the Amex.

SBOTOP
AMERICAN EXPRESS
20
10
7
30
betway

.com
AMERICAN EXP
COMMUNITY S
SUSSEX ASPHALTE
WOODHART GROUP
mexmast
SeatGeek
TROSSARD
11
13
25
30
SBOTOP
18
SOCCER 2022

Pre-Match Ryhme

It's a full house at the Amex,
Always a fantastic sight.
I wonder if the away support,
Are still annoyed about Ben White?

I'm feeling pretty confident,
Which may sound a tad conceited.
But if we lose, the great thing is,
This rhyme can be deleted.

In-Match Rhymes

1m: KICK-OFF

Leeds at our place,
The Amex is packed.
Three points from the game,
Let's now extract.

↓

1m: GROSS CLATTERED

A bash in the head,
For Der Kaiser.
As to who was the culprit,
I think he's none the wiser.

↓

14m: WEBSTER HEADS WIDE

A Purvis cross,
Webster onside.
But his header?
Flies just wide.

↓

17m: WEBSTER HEADS WIDE (AGAIN!)

Free-kick from Gross,
Lovely curler.
Webster heads wide,
Just like minutes earlier.

↓

27m: SWING AND A MISS

Unusual from Leo,
Who lacks composure.
With his weaker left foot,
He scoops one over.

30m: MARCH TESTS THE KEEPER

Solly through,
Defenders harried.
Left-foot shot,
Keeper parried.

↓

31m: OLD SCHOOL COMMENTATOR

I haven't heard that phrase,
For a while.
"Solly's burning down the wing",
That made me smile.

↓

45m: SANCHEZ SAVE

James' cross came in,
Leeds persist.
Rob palms it away,
Strong right wrist.

↓

HALF-TIME RHYME

Some advice, Graham,
If I can.
Tell the boys they're at Old Trafford,
Or West Ham.

↓

48m: CHANCE FOR GROSS

Such great play,
Oh, so deft.
Chance for Pascal,
Flies just left.

54m: SOLLY DENIED

Danny involved,
Gross was too.
Keeper saves,
But Solly was through!

↓

60m: CONSTANT PRESSURE

Is it as apparent to you,
As it is to me.
We don't want a point,
And are going for three?

↓

66m: PASCAL PUTS US IN FRONT!!!!! (1-0)

Finally, a goal,
Scored by us.
We're 1-0 up,
What was the fuss?

↓

76m: MARSCH BOOKED

The Leeds manager,
Goes in the book.
His emotions,
Overcooked.

↓

90+3m: FINAL WHISTLE

We win 1-0,
Pascal scores.
At the final whistle,
THE NORTH STAND ROARS!!

Post-Match Ryhme

Leeds United at the Amex,
Is never an easy tie.
I would have settled for a point today,
I'm not going to lie.

Four games down, 10 points claimed,
It honestly feels a bit absurd.
But we'll raise a glass to our club,
Because tonight, we're sitting third.

MATCH #6

Tuesday, 30 August 2022

Fulham 2 – 1 Brighton & Hove Albion

Competition: **Premier League**
Kick-off: **19.30**
Venue: **Craven Cottage, London**
Weather: **20c, part cloudy**
Referee: **Thomas Bramall**
Attendance: **22,224**

Squads

Fulham: Leno, Tete, Tosin, Ream, Robinson, Reed (Chalobah 92), João Palhinha, Kebano, Andreas Pereira (Cairney 78), De Cordova-Reid, Mitrović. **Unused subs:** Ablade, Francois, Stansfield, Harris, Mbabu, Rodák, Diop.

Albion: Sanchez, Veltman (Lamptey 62), Dunk, Webster, Estupinan (Mitoma 62), Mac Allister, Caicedo (Undav 78), Trossard, Mwepu (Welbeck 62), Gross, March. **Unused subs:** Steele, Colwill, Alzate, Enciso, van Hecke.

Match Preview

Our fifth Premier League game of the season took us to the banks of the Thames in west London and the pleasant surrounds of Fulham's Craven Cottage.

Over the last couple of decades, and under different ownership, there had been speculation that the highly desirable plot of land on which this compact ground sat would get sold. But with a new main stand built, it seemed Fulham were committed to staying in this most picturesque of locations for the long-term.

Having briefly led the table during our 1-0 win over Leeds the previous week, we started the game in fourth place with ten points from four games.

Fulham had made a solid start to their campaign following promotion. Although Marco Silva's side had lost to Arsenal the previous week, they had managed a win over Brentford and draws against Liverpool and Wolves, too. With their Serbian striker Aleksandar Mitrovic in a good run of form, it was likely to be a challenging game.

Adam Lallana had been ruled out until the end of September with a calf problem, and there was some doubt over Joel Veltman, who had been suffering from a stiff neck. Jeremy Sarmiento was back in training but wouldn't be risked, and Jakub Moder was still absent.

It was a mild and still night in London – perfect for a game of football.

MAC ALLISTER
10
8
AMERICAN EXPRESS
NIKE

Energizer
AMERICAN EXPRESS

Pre-Match Ryhme

We're heading north to London,
In high spirits and good voice.
Hoping that as the final whistle blows,
We can celebrate and rejoice.

It's not long since our last game,
We hope the boys aren't too fatigued.
As if we win, you won't believe the size of my grin,
As we might even top the league.

In-Match Rhymes

1m: KICK-OFF

And we're off,
Looking bright.
As we're playing away,
It's crimson tonight,

↓

7m: DANGER AVERTED

A quick break by Fulham,
A march they stole.
Fizzing low cross,
Put out by Joel.

↓

8m: ROB'S BIG HANDS

The resulting corner,
Didn't hear a shout.
Rob, with his left hand,
Palms it out.

↓

16m: CHANGE IN TACTICS

Early Fulham pressure,
And whilst there's no score.
Graham switches,
To a back four.

↓

28m: FIRST EFFORT FOR ALBION

Gross and Moises,
Lovely move.
We're looking good,
I approve.

38m: MARCH HEADS WIDE

Gross to Leo,
Who swings one in.
Solly heads wide,
Takes it on the chin.

↓

HALF-TIME RHYME

Got to be honest,
Sloppy game.
Not just us,
They're the same.

↓

48m: MITROVIC SCORES (1-0)

Fulham short corner,
The ball isn't cleared.
Mitrovic strikes,
He's the guy we feared.

↓

55m: DUNK OWN GOAL (2-0)

Pervis caught,
A night to forget?
And yet they've not,
Looked much of a threat.

↓

58m: PENALTY TO ALBION!

VAR check,
Pen awarded.
Pervis tripped,
Our attack rewarded.

60m: GOAL! (2-1)

Alexis scores,
From the spot.
For now, we've managed to,
Stop the rot.

↓

62m: CLOSE FOR THE HOME SIDE

Sanchez fumbles,
That was just bizarre.
The resulting shot,
Somehow clears the bar.

↓

71m: LAST 20 MINUTES

Pushing forward
Now in waves.
Left-foot shot from Leo,
Their keeper saves.

↓

80m: CLOSE FOR UNDAV

Behind the back four,
Undav ghosts.
But his little chip,
Hits the post.

↓

90+6m: FINAL WHISTLE

For the first time this season,
It's a bit of a 'fail'.
Couldn't grab a second goal,
To get out of jail.

Post-Match Ryhme

We were hoping to top the table,
At least, that was our aim.
We huffed and puffed and tried our best,
But we could not win the game.

I wonder what it is about Fulham,
They're becoming our bogey team.
As we're yet to beat them in five Premier League games,
And now I need a beer to let off steam.

MATCH #7

Sunday, 4 September 2022

Brighton & Hove Albion 5 – 2 Leicester City

Competition: **Premier League**
Kick-off: **14.00**
Venue: **The Amex Stadium, Brighton**
Weather: **22c, sunny**
Referee: **Tony Harrington**
Attendance: **31,185**

Squads

Albion: Sanchez, Veltman, Dunk, Webster, Mac Allister, Trossard (Estupinan 89), Mwepu (Undav 83), Caicedo (Gilmour 90+2), Gross, March (Lamptey 90+3), Welbeck. **Unused subs:** Steele, Colwill, Alzate, Mitoma, van Hecke.

Leicester City: Ward, Justin, Ndidi, Evans, Thomas, Maddison, Soumaré (Dewsbury-Hall 72), Tielemans (Amartey 72), Barnes (Castagne 45), Iheanacho (Vardy 72), Daka. **Unused subs:** Albrighton, Pérez, Mendy, Praet, Iversen.

Match Preview

Following our first defeat of the season five days earlier, we were looking to bounce back against Leicester on this balmy Sunday afternoon at the Amex.

While our good start to the campaign has raised anticipation levels, Leicester's season had yet to get going. Following defeat to Manchester United in their fifth game, Brendan Rodgers' side sat at the bottom of the Premier League table with just one point. Surprisingly to some, they had let their keeper and captain Kasper Schmeichel join French side Nice the previous month whilst also selling their highly-rated centre-back Wesley Fofana to Chelsea.

Key players for Leicester included James Maddison, who had already scored twice and got an assist this season as he continued the excellent form he produced in the second half of the 2021/22 campaign. With 20 goal involvements (12 goals, eight assists) the previous season, the England international would no doubt be a vital creative outlet for the Foxes again.

Despite his lack of playing time, Graham Potter confirmed that new signing Billy Gilmour was available for selection and that, although Veltman, Sarmiento and Lallana weren't, their fitness issues weren't likely to be long-term.

It was a beautiful and sunny late summer's day at the Amex for this thriller of a match.

BET
UNIB
FBS
trade online
AMERICAN EXPRESS
.com

FBS
trade online
AMERICAN
EXPRESS
UNIBET

Pre-Match Ryhme

Last week was a bad day at the office,
Tuesday night away.
So I'm glad we're back at the Amex,
Where we've put on some great displays.

Danny Welbeck is fit and starts,
Bringing experience and pace.
We'd all like to see him get a goal,
In fact, why not make it a brace?

In-Match Rhymes

1m: KICK-OFF

The sun is out,
The sky is blue.
Here we go,
Three points we pursue.

↓

1m: EARLY GOAL FOR LEICESTER (0-1)

Less than a minute gone,
My eyes deceivin'.
Leicester score!
I'm not believin'.

↓

10m: EQUALISER!!! (1-1)

Lovely cross-field ball,
To Leo from Gross.
Lobs it in for Solly,
At the back post!

↓

12m: SIMULATION!

Alexis booked,
Man, alive.
Maddison faking,
He took a dive!

↓

15m: MOISES PUTS US IN FRONT!! (2-1)

Mwepu breaks,
Various options wide.
Chooses Moises,
WE'VE TURNED THE TIDE!!!

33m: LEICESTER LEVEL (2-2)

Leicester level,
Madisson's long ball through.
Dunk left on his backside,
This can't be true!

↓

42m: SANCHEZ SAVE!

Harvey Barnes,
Puts himself about.
Powerful right-foot shot,
But Rob palms it out.

↓

HALF-TIME RHYME

I think we can all agree,
With what's being said.
And that's an early second-half goal,
Puts the game to bed.

↓

47m: AN ALEXIS THUNDERBOLT

Oh, my word!
Pick that one out!
A Mac Allister worldly,
Oh wait, VAR rules it out.

↓

64m: LEO PUTS US AHEAD!!! (3-2)

Bottom right-hand corner,
What a star!
And this one's not chalked off,
By VAR.

68m: SHOULD BE 4-2!

Great work by Gross,
Forward we poured.
Stinging shot by Solly,
Saved by Ward.

↓

70m: PENALTY TO US!

Oh yes, Leo,
Twinkle toes.
Clumsy tackle,
Down he goes.

↓

71m: GOAL!!! PEN CONVERTED BY ALEXIS!! (4-2)

There's no one better,
A pen to take.
Right down the middle,
No mistake.

↓

90+7m: WOW! GOAL! ALEXIS!! (5-2)

What a free-kick!!!
And after the earlier farse.
VAR can stick that one,
UP THEIR.......!!!

↓

90+9m: FINAL WHISTLE

Bloody hell,
What a match!
Alexis Mac Allister,
What a catch!

Post-Match Ryhme

Whilst it wasn't the best start to the game,
We fought back to claim the win.
As for what VAR is doing to football,
I don't know where to begin.

We end the game in fourth place,
With an impressive 13 points from six.
And whilst I hope I don't have to eat my words,
By May, we'll be pushing for Europe, I predicts.

MATCH #8

Saturday, 1 October 2022

Liverpool 3 – 3 Brighton & Hove Albion

Competition: **Premier League**
Kick-off: **15.00**
Venue: **Anfield, Liverpool**
Weather: **17c, sunny**
Referee: **Andy Madley**
Attendance: **53,320**

Squads

Liverpool: Alisson, Alexander-Arnold, Matip, van Dijk, Tsimikas (Milner 58), Henderson (Elliott 59), Fabinho, Thiago Alcántara (Núñez 89), Salah, Firmino (Jota 75), Carvalho (Díaz 45). **Unused subs:** Gomez, Adrián, Arthur, Phillips.

Albion: Sanchez, Veltman, Webster, Dunk, Estupinan (Lallana 75), March, Caicedo, Mac Allister, Gross (Mitoma 64), Trossard (Lamptey 86), Welbeck. **Unused subs:** Steele, Colwill, Sarmiento, Enciso, Undav, Gilmour.

Match Preview

Who could have guessed?

Surely no one could have imagined when we beat Leicester at the Amex that it would be almost four weeks until we played our next game and that we'd have a new head coach in charge when we did.

But that's where we found ourselves.

Whilst the passing of Her Majesty Queen Elizabeth II had led to the postponement of most top-flight football, we'd suffered a loss far closer to home as following Thomas Tuchel's departure, Graham Potter had accepted an invitation to join Chelsea as head coach.

Therefore, it was our newly appointed head coach Roberto De Zerbi took charge of our visit to Anfield, and with Spurs, Manchester City, and Chelsea amongst our next five opponents, it promised to be a baptism of fire for the Italian. However, having won four of our opening six league games, he would have no doubt been hoping to continue the fine start to the campaign we'd made under Potter.

Jurgen Klopp's men had experienced a mixed start to the campaign with two wins, three draws and a loss from their opening six games.

Although Mwepu was unavailable, unsurprisingly, De Zerbi fielded a familiar line-up.

It was a glorious day on Merseyside for this fantastic match.

MERICAN
EXPRESS
HENDERS
14
4
standard
chartered

MARCH
7
AMERICAN EXPRESS

Pre-Match Ryhme

Our new manager is called Roberto,
As Graham has left us for pastures new.
Shame he took most of his backroom staff,
It's left us in a stew.

But the club is so well run,
It's clear for all to see.
These things happen, life moves on,
And that the board have a great plan B.

In-Match Rhymes

1m KICK-OFF

Perfect pitch,
Sun low in the sky.
We're in blue & white,
And Roberto's our guy

↓

4m: TROSSARD PUTS US AHEAD!!! (0-1)

Bloody hell,
What do you reckon?
Ahead after only three minutes,
And 48 seconds!!

↓

5m: WOW!

We pushed forward,
Their defence did part.
Roberto De Zerbi,
WHAT A START!

↓

10m: ALISSON SAVES FROM WELBECK!!

Solly's cross,
Danny is free.
Downward header,
Goodness me.

↓

13m: ALISSON SAVES AGAIN

We're on fire,
Running riot.
Leandro Trossard,
They can't keep him quiet.

17m: TROSSARD DOUBLES THE LEAD (0-2)

Liverpool's defenders,
If looks could kill.
It's Leo again,
AND IT'S TWO NIL!

↓

31m: BLOCK BY SANCHEZ

Salah though,
Sanchez brave.
Dives at his feet,
Super save.

↓

33m: LIVERPOOL GET ONE BACK (1-2)

Messy goal,
Initially disallowed.
VAR overturns,
Pleasing the home crowd.

↓

HALF-TIME RHYME

If we don't win this
It will be a crime.
Some of our play
Is just sublime.

↓

54m: FIRMINO EQUALISES (2-2)

One minute we're looking,
A real threat.
But 20 seconds later,
The ball's in our net.

63m: LIVERPOOL TAKE THE LEAD (3-2)

Corner comes in,
Sanchez not in control.
Punches the ball,
Onto Webster, own goal.

↓

74m: DANNY CLOSE WITH A HEADER

Mitoma crosses,
What a run.
Danny is there,
But so is Aliss-un.

↓

83m: YES!! TROSSARD EQUALISES!!! (3-3)

Mitoma again,
Crosses from the left.
It's a Trossard hat-trick,
Liverpool bereft.

↓

90+5m: HUGE SAVE FROM SANCHEZ

Man, that was close,
Alexander-Arnold free-kick.
Heading for the bottom corner,
But for Rob's tiny flick.

↓

90+7m: FINAL WHISTLE

Two early goals by Leo,
Liverpool fought back.
Although for their third,
Rob might get some flack.

Post-Match Ryhme

We headed up to Anfield,
And with Liverpool went toe to toe.
Left with a point, although it could have been three,
If it wasn't for Firmino.

It leaves us tonight in fourth place,
Things are looking very healthy.
We've got fourteen points from seven games,
And are one place above Potter's Chelsea.

MATCH #9

Saturday, 8 October 2022

Brighton & Hove Albion 0 – 1 Tottenham Hotspur

Competition: **Premier League**
Kick-off: **17.30**
Venue: **The Amex Stadium, Brighton**
Weather: **15c, bright**
Referee: **Tony Harrington**
Attendance: **31,498**

Squads

Albion: Sanchez, Veltman (Lamptey 88), Webster, Dunk, Estupinan (Mitoma 66), Caicedo (Gilmour 88), Mac Allister, Gross (Lallana 81), Trossard, Welbeck, March. **Unused subs:** Steele, Colwill, Sarmiento, Undav, Turns.

Spurs: Lloris, Romero, Dier, Davies, Doherty, Bentancur, Bissouma (Richarlison 70), Højbjerg, R Sessegnon, Son Heung-min (Perisicat 80), Kane (Skipp 90). **Unused subs:** D Sánchez, Gil, Perisic, Forster, Spence, Sarr, Lenget.

Match Preview

After the previous weekend's six-goal thriller against Liverpool that had maintained our fourth-place position, our home match against Spurs represented Roberto De Zerbi's first opportunity to experience the atmosphere at the Amex as we welcomed Antonio Conte's side in a late afternoon kick-off.

With Mwepu still unavailable, De Zerbi's main injury concern was Caicedo. However, he was hopeful Moises would be able to start whilst no doubt also hoping we could repeat the 1-0 victory we enjoyed at the Tottenham Hotspur Stadium when we last met.

Despite a derby-day defeat to Arsenal at the Emirates the previous week, Spurs sat fourth (three points & one place above us) entering the match with 17 points from eight games and included Yves Bissouma in their line-up after he'd signed for Spurs from us in the summer.

Tottenham's Harry Kane would be the usual threat. He had become the first player to score 100 away goals in the Premier League in their defeat against Arsenal. He'd also scored five goals in his last seven Premier League games against us, including three in four at the Amex.

The fixture promised to be an emotional occasion for Spurs' management, backroom staff, players, and fans with the passing of Tottenham fitness coach Gian Piero Ventrone a few days earlier.

It was a pleasant autumnal afternoon on the Sussex coast - although things didn't quite go as we'd hoped.

HØJBJERG
5
UNIBET
AIA
AIA
30
11

AMERICAN EXPRESS
10
VELTMAN
34
SON
7
4
Captain
raizer
15
AMERICAN EXPRESS
DOHERTY
2

Pre-Match Ryhme

I hope you make the kick-off,
As I hear at Brighton Station, there's a queue.
At least it's set for perfect weather,
For Roberto's home debut.

Let's hope after 90 minutes,
We've got all three points in the bag,
As a win against this lot is something,
About which I'd really like to brag.

In-Match Rhymes

0m: PAYING RESPECTS

Before we kick-off,
An emotional pause.
For Gian Piero,
A minute's applause.

↓

1m: KICK-OFF

Here we go,
A bright and sunny day.
But not that warm,
Winter's not far away.

↓

3m: FREE-KICK TO SPURS

Harry Kane,
Down again.
Defensive discipline,
We must maintain.

↓

4m: SAVE BY SANCHEZ

Son's free kick,
Up over the wall.
Rob dives to his right,
And diverts the ball.

↓

10m: A LET OFF

Spurs advance down the left,
A Sessegnon cross.
But lucky for us,
Doherty's connection's dross.

21m: SANCHEZ SAVES FROM BENTANCUR!

One for the cameras?
Not one bit.
Super left-handed save,
After a super hit.

↓

22m: GOAL FOR SPURS (0-1)

Resulting corner,
We don't clear.
Harry Kane header,
It's what we feared.

↓

36m: DUNK HEADS JUST OVER THE BAR!

Our third corner,
In a row.
The ball flies high,
When we needed low.

↓

44m: SAVE FROM LLORIS

It's a decent shot,
From our Danny.
But the result,
Is a Hugo parry.

↓

HALF-TIME RHYME

Spurs are a little sharper,
It seems to me.
Big half-time talk,
Coming from De Zerbi.

67m: MITOMA COMES ON

Pervis off,
Kaoru on.
The Japanese fans go wild,
Who've come along.

↓

68m: MITOMA CAUSES HAVOC!

What a dribble,
Kaoru beats three!
Lloris smothers,
Goodness me.

↓

74m: DISALLOWED GOAL FOR SPURS

Decent finish,
But for Son a drag.
It's ruled out,
Via the lino's flag.

↓

78m: DANNY WITH SPACE, PULLS IT WIDE

Left-foot shot,
Edge of the box.
Spurs defenders avoid Danny,
Like he's got chickenpox.

↓

90+5m: FINAL WHISTLE

The whistle goes,
We lose at home.
Down to sixth,
A collective groan.

Post-Match Ryhme

We weren't entirely on form today,
I feel we were slightly off the pace.
It's a result which means, unfortunately,
We dropped out of a Champions League place.

Maybe we were too tippy-tappy,
In the area, oh, it smarts.
One thing we learnt from the last 23 minutes?
Next time, Mitoma starts!

MATCH #10

Friday, 14 October 2022

Brentford 2 – 0 Brighton & Hove Albion

Competition: **Premier League**
Kick-off: **20.00**
Venue: **The Gtech Community Stadium, Brentford**
Weather: **14c, clear**
Referee: **Michael Salisbury**
Attendance: **17, 016**

Squads

Brentford: Raya, Ajer, Pinnock, Mee, Henry (Ghoddos 87), Janelt, Onyeka (Baptiste 71), Jensen (Dasilva 80), Mbeumo (Canós 80), Wissa (Roerslev 71), Toney. **Unused subs:** Cox, Zanka, Lewis-Potter, Damsgaard.

Albion: Sanchez, Veltman, Dunk, Webster, Estupinan (Mitoma 46), Mac Allister, Caicedo, Gross (Lallana 68) March, Trossard (Undav 68), Welbeck. **Unused subs:** Steele, Lamptey, Sarmiento, Enciso, Gilmour, Turns.

Match Preview

Everyone associated with the club had been shocked and saddened on hearing the news that Enock Mwepu had been forced to retire with a heart condition, and I am sure the team had him in their thoughts as they headed up to London for this rare Friday night game.

Roberto De Zerbi had yet to taste victory as our new head coach, having taken a point at Anfield before suffering a home defeat to Spurs in our previous game. He reported no new injury concerns as we aimed to move back into the top four. Sitting seventh with 14 points, we knew victory would put us above Chelsea and into fourth spot, whilst Brentford would move to within a point of us should they secure all three points.

Albion had generally enjoyed our away days so far, winning twice and drawing once in our four matches on the road, but we faced a tough test against a Brentford side who had taken seven of their 10 Premier League points at home.

Whilst we'd managed the double over Brentford last season, Thomas Frank's side had earned plenty of praise in their first season in the Premier League, and with in-form Ivan Toney up front, it promised to be a tough fixture.

And so it proved to be.

HOLLYWOOD bets
AMERICAN EXPRESS
AMERICAN EXPRESS
bet365

Pre-Match Ryhme

I can't wait to see Kaoru Mitoma,
Running down the line.
Their defender, left for dead,
Each and every time.

I hope tonight he's not just an 'impact sub',
As I think he can offer so much more.
So I'm looking forward to seeing him involved,
Along with new signing, Billy Gilmour.

In-Match Rhymes

0m: THE COMPUTER

We will miss Enock's goals,
We will miss his grin.
Just happy he's in good hands,
And that he's still plugged in.

↓

1m: KICK-OFF

There's no Amex without Tony,
Let's not pretend.
Great to see our chairman,
In the away end.

↓

4m: EARLY BRENTFORD CHANCE

We've been pinned back,
In the game so far.
Early Brentford chance,
Flies over the bar.

↓

16m: ALBION PUSHING

Danny Welbeck,
Two early shouts.
Right-foot, then a header,
Their keeper keeps them out,

↓

18m: AND BREATH

This looks like a Brentford side,
Bang on form.
But hopefully, we've weathered,
The early storm.

20m: MOISES – ALMOST!

Moises Caicedo,
Oh, behave!
Stinging right-foot shot,
Fingertip save.

↓

21m: SAVED FROM JOEL

The resulting corner,
Solly fires in.
Veltman shoots,
Away support makes a din.

↓

27m: BRENTFORD AHEAD (1-0)

Three Brentford players,
All combined.
Toney finishes,
And we're behind.

↓

44m: BOTH MANAGERS GET BOOKED

Thomas Frank stops Veltman,
Taking a throw.
Things get messy,
Tempers grow.

↓

HALF-TIME RHYME

Toney's making decisions,
On the ref's behalf.
At least two goals needed,
In the second half.

62m: PENALTY TO BRENTFORD

Veltman catches Toney,
Right or not.
Ref says "yes",
And points to the spot.

↓

63m: GOAL TO BRENTFORD (0-2)

We're 2-0 down,
But not a poor display.
Toney steps up,
Seems it's not our day.

↓

68m: MARCH GOES CLOSE!

Mitoma to March,
Free header six yards out.
Keeper makes the save,
Again, we go without.

↓

86m: NOW DUNK GOES CLOSE!

On another day,
We could be level.
And get a bit more praise,
From Sky's Gary Neville.

↓

90+6m: FINAL WHISTLE

Decent performance,
But disappointing night.
But on the plus side,
Enock's alright.

Post-Match Ryhme

A full 73% possession,
That is what the stats say we had.
Including 28 shots and 11 corners,
We honestly didn't play that bad.

But the only stat that counts,
Is the one that reads two goals to nil.
Tonight we're having to swallow,
A really bitter pill.

MATCH #11

Tuesday, 18 October 2022

Brighton & Hove Albion 0 – 0 Nottingham Forest

Competition: **Premier League**
Kick-off: **19.30**
Venue: **The Amex Stadium, Brighton**
Weather: **13c, clear**
Referee: **Darren England**
Attendance: **31, 463**

Squads

Albion: Sanchez, Veltman, Dunk, Webster, Trossard, Mac Allister, Caicedo, Gross (Undav 85), March, Lallana (Lamptey 64), Welbeck. **Unused subs:** Steele, Van Hecke, Estupinan, Turns, Gilmour, Sarmiento, Enciso.

Nottingham Forest: Henderson, Aurier (Toffolo 69, Biancone 86), S Cook, McKenna, N Williams, Yates, Freuler, Mangala (Kouyaté 61), Gibbs-White, Johnson (Awoniyi 86), Lingard, (Worrall 86). **Unused subs:** Hennessey, Surridge, Dennis, Boly.

Match Preview

After two consecutive defeats, and with our new head coach still looking for his first win, we were hoping to bounce back against Nottingham Forest under the lights at the Amex.

Steve Cooper's Forest had experienced a poor start to the season since their long-awaited return to the Premier League. After ten games, they sat bottom with just five points despite a considerable influx of players since they secured promotion at the end of the previous season.

One of these players was Morgan Gibbs-White, who had become Forest's record signing when he joined them in the summer for a reported £25 million fee with add-ons. The England under-21 international had started all but one of his new side's Premier League games but was yet to score.

Despite their poor start, the Reds had shown their faith in Steve Cooper, recently handing him a new contract after guiding Forest back to the top-flight for the first time since 1999.

It was our first game against Forest in quite a few years. As Albion closed in on promotion to the Premier League, we'd suffered an unexpected slip-up, as a Zach Clough brace and a goal from Ben Osborn condemned us to a 3-0 defeat in March 2017.

Roberto confirmed that Adam Lallana would be starting but that Kaoru Mitoma would miss out after picking up an ankle injury against Brentford.

I was back in Sussex and at the Amex for this one.

Although I didn't choose the best match.

Premier League
BRIGHTON & HOVE
YATES
22
AMERICAN EXPRESS

Pre-Match Ryhme

We're back under the lights at the Amex,
Haven't played Forest in the Premier League before.
And if you look at the table,
You should be able to predict the score.

But things are rarely that simple,
Recent results haven't gone as we'd wished.
And whilst Roberto's yet to win, here's the thing,
He's a man that you just can't resist.

In-Match Rhymes

0m: DISCO FEVER?

I know some are unsure,
But I have to say.
I enjoyed,
The light display.

↓

1m: KICK-OFF

It's a bit nippy,
But what a sight.
A full Amex,
Under lights.

↓

5m: A BRIGHT START FROM WELBECK

I know he's too young,
To be called a sage.
But Danny runs like a man,
Who's half his age.

↓

13m: CLOSE!

Trossard v Henderson,
Shot from the former.
The latter palms it over,
And the result is a corner.

↓

18m: PROMISING FROM MARCH

Solly breaks forward,
After a mistake at the back.
But Forest defend in numbers,
It's a cul-de-sac.

23m: FOREST FINDING THEIR FEET

Haven't tested,
Sanchez yet.
But they're looking,
More of a threat.

↓

30m: LEO HITS THE BAR!

Great right-foot volley,
Great build-up play.
Top right-hand corner,
On another day.

↓

33m: HENDERSON SAVES FROM SOLLY

The bottom right-hand corner,
Was Solly's plan.
But it's a save low to his left,
From the ex-Man U man.

↓

35m: GROSS AND WELBECK DENIED

It's their keeper again,
Two saves in succession.
We've still yet to register,
Despite all our possession.

↓

45m: WEBSTER FIRES IT OVER

Pulled back by Gross,
But a chance.
Looked offside to me,
At first glance.

HALF-TIME RHYME

So many chances,
We're creating.
None going in,
So frustrating.

↓

51m: WELBECK NODS WIDE

Lovely cross from Veltman,
Danny is free.
We're yet to score,
But could have had three.

↓

64m: TARIQ ON FOR LALLANA

Lamptey on,
What a sight.
Just a speedy blur,
Of blue & white.

↓

81m: PASCAL SCUFFS A GREAT CHANCE

Lamptey crosses,
Flick from Danny,
Falls to Gross,
Who hits it like my granny.

↓

90+5m: FINAL WHISTLE

We were all hoping for,
One final shout.
But nothing doing,
The game peters out.

Post-Match Ryhme

When I make it back to the Amex,
Our record isn't good.
Whenever I'm able to make the trip,
We don't win when, arguably, we should.

Tonight was one of those occasions,
We failed to get the three points that we sought,
But fear not, Albion fans, as I've some good news,
The chances of me making it back again this year are nought.

MATCH #12

Saturday, 22 October 2022

Manchester City 3 – 1 Brighton & Hove Albion

Competition: **Premier League**
Kick-off: **15:00**
Venue: **The Etihad Stadium, Manchester**
Weather: **16c, bright**
Referee: **Craig Pawson**
Attendance: **53,223**

Squads

Manchester City: Ederson, Akanji, Dias, Laporte, Cancelo, Rodrigo, De Bruyne, Bernardo, Mahrez (Foden 61), Grealish (Palmer 77), Haaland (Alvarez 80). **Unused subs:** Ortega Moreno, Stones, Ake, Gundogan, Gomez, Lewis.

Albion: Sanchez; Veltman (Estupinan 65), Dunk, Webster; March, Mac Allister (Gilmour 86), Caicedo, Trossard; Gross (Sarmiento 86), Lallana (Lamptey 45); Welbeck (Undav 78). **Unused subs:** Steele, Colwill, Enciso, van Hecke.

Match Preview

Having picked up only one point in three games, heading to the Etihad to play the current Premier League champions isn't a fixture anyone would choose. However, the mood was generally positive amongst supporters as the consensus seemed to be that there were plenty of positive signs that indicated our new manager could make a real impact.

Having drawn with Liverpool and Nottingham Forest whilst suffering defeats to Tottenham and Brentford, we headed to Manchester in eighth place in the Premier League with 15 points. However, we were still looking for our first win under Roberto De Zerbi.

As far as City were concerned, having won seven of their opening 11 games, Pep Guardiola's side sat second - four points off Arsenal in top spot — but they had also suffered their first defeat of the season at Liverpool the previous weekend. However, with striker Erling Haaland who they had signed from Borussia Dortmund in June, they also had a phenomenal goal-scorer who had already netted 15 times in the season.

Injury-wise, De Zerbi had indicated that Kaoru Mitoma and Levi Colwill would need to be assessed but other than long-term injuries, there were no new issues.

It was a predictably tough day.

AMERICAN
EXPRESS
25

7
9
13

27

Pre-Match Ryhme

If you are an Albion fan,
Then, no doubt, like me,
You're hoping the gap of eight points,
Will soon be reduced by three.

Guardiola has been very complimentary,
About Roberto and our club,
Thank you Pep, but we'd prefer a favour,
How about you name Haarland as a sub?

In-Match Rhymes

1m: KICK-OFF

The sun is out,
The sky is blue.
And I'm predicting,
A draw, 2-2.

↓

7m: WELBECK IS DOWN

Treatment for Danny,
Flailing arm in the eye?
As my mum used to say,
"You aren't going to die".

↓

11m: GOOD CHANCE FOR WELBECK

Let off for City,
Danny tried,
To lob their keeper,
But it goes well wide.

↓

19m: CITY DENIED A PENALTY

Does Sanchez catch Haarland?
Either way, down he goes.
VAR takes a look,
I've seen them given those.

↓

22m: CITY SCORE (1-0)

It's route one from their keeper,
And Haarland scores it.
A clear shove on Webster,
But the ref ignores it.

30m: ? COME ON JACK

I think Grealish,
Is a decent bloke.
But going down like?
What a joke.

↓

32m: DUNK BLOCKS FROM DE BRUYNE

City sweep forward,
A decent move.
Great block by our captain,
Roberto approves.

↓

42m: PEN TO CITY

So, if you leave your leg out,
And bump into your man,
A penalty will be given?
VAR is a sham.

↓

43m: CITY SCORE (2-0)

Haarland scores,
Man, that's tough.
One was bound to be given,
They've claimed enough.

↓

HALF-TIME RHYME

City ahead,
And in control.
We desperately need,
An early second-half goal.

53m: TROSSARD SCORES!!! (2-1)

Into the edge of the area,
Our Leo ghosts.
And hits a powerful right-foot strike,
Inside the near post!!!!

↓

67m: ALBION PUSHING

Strong spell,
From us.
City forced,
To park the bus.

↓

73m: EDERSON DENIES TROSSARD

It was a great opportunity,
So the chances were slim.
But Danny is still furious,
That Leo didn't pull it back for him.

↓

75m: STUNNER FROM DE BRUYNE (3-1)

We had our chances,
But didn't score.
Punished with a goal,
From the top drawer.

↓

90+4m: FINAL WHISTLE

We stood with the Champions,
Toe-to-toe.
Promising signs,
On we go.

Post-Match Ryhme

Is he a human or a robot?
It's sometimes hard to be completely sure.
But Erling Haarland is setting records,
And I don't think it's premature.

To suggest he may score more this season,
Than any striker there's even been.
I don't usually do rhymes about the opposition,
But the guy is a machine.

MATCH #13

Saturday, 29 October 2022

Brighton & Hove Albion 4 – 1 Chelsea

Competition: **Premier League**
Kick-off: **15:00**
Venue: **The Amex Stadium, Brighton**
Weather: **20c, bright**
Referee: **Andy Madley**
Attendance: **31,746**

Squads

Albion: Sanchez, Gross, Webster, Dunk, Estupinan, Caicedo, Mac Allister, March, Lallana (Enciso 65), Mitoma (Lamptey 72), Trossard (Sarmiento 86). **Unused subs:** Steele, Undav, Gilmour, Turns, Furlong, Moran.

Chelsea: Kepa (Mendy 46'), Chalobah, Thiago Silva (c), Cucurella (Chilwell 64'), Pulisic (Broja, 79'), Kovacic, Loftus-Cheek, Sterling ((Aubameyang 64'), Mount, Gallagher (Ziyech 79'), Havertz. **Unused subs:** Azpilicueta, Jorginho, Zakaria, Hutchinson.

Match Preview

Here it was. The big one!

Just over seven weeks after leaving us and replacing Thomas Tuchel as head coach at Chelsea, Graham Potter was back at the Amex with his new club. It had been a painful time for us fans as Potter also took numerous back-room staff, including club legend Bruno.

However, whilst emotions were running high at the Amex, I believed we'd be better off focusing on supporting the lads rather than giving Potter a piece of our minds. But I'm not sure how many shared that view!

From our perspective, whilst still waiting for our first win under Roberto De Zerbi, we went into the game sitting ninth and having witnessed some promising signs — including in our defeat to Manchester City the previous week.

The pre-match stats suggested things might not change in this regard as not only had Potter's reign at Chelsea started well (they were unbeaten under him coming into the match), but, in 10 attempts, we had yet to beat Chelsea in the Premier League (D4 L6).

The main team news was that Joel Veltman (calf) was doubtful, but that Kaoru Mitoma and Adam Lallana were back in training and were likely to be available for selection.

What a game! What an atmosphere! What a result!

UNIBET
UNIBET
11
17
10

Pre-Match Ryhme

Not long ago, someone deserted us,
Our ex-coach, Graham Potter.
He took many of his backroom staff too,
A polite description would be a "rotter".

But to abuse a guy who chose a better-paid job,
Is personally, I think a little rich.
WE are the fans, remember he was just the coach,
How about we do our talking on the pitch?

In-Match Rhymes

1m: KICK-OFF

There's no way this,
Will be a 0-0 draw.
Never heard the Amex,
Like this before!

↓

2m: OH, MARC

Last season he was,
Our favourite fella.
But just listen to the boos,
For Marc Cucurella!

↓

3m: TWO GOAL-LINE CLEARANCES!

First a chip from Leo,
Silva stretching on his toes.
And then another from Pervis,
Wide it goes!

↓

5m: LEO SCORES!!!!! (1-0)

Chelsea at the back,
What are they doing?
Left-footed from Trossard,
UPSET BREWING!!

↓

6m: WHAT. A. NOISE!!!!

Nicely set up,
By Kaoru Mitoma.
I can hear the north stand,
AND I'M IN OKLAHOMA!!!

14m: CHELSEA OWN GOAL!! (2-0)

If you study the replay,
I think you'll see.
That's a Chelsea OG,
Off Loftus-Cheek's knee!!!!

↓

18m: SAVE BY SANCHEZ

My huge relief,
I just can't hide.
Rob saves from Gallagher,
Pulisic fires wide.

↓

20m: ROB DENIES GALLAGHER AGAIN

Whipped in from Sterling,
But let's keep calm.
Heading for the top right-hand corner,
Saved by Rob's palm.

↓

31m: CAICEDO HITS THE SIDE NETTING

3 - 0 to the Albion?
Well, almost.
In fact, I think Moises' shot,
Actually skims the post.

↓

42m: CHALOBAH WITH ANOTHER OG!! (3-0)

It was crossed by Pervis,
He's the best.
Thank you, Trevoh,
IT'S A GOAL-FEST!

HALF-TIME RHYME

Chelsea scored two,
But incredibly, still.
Albion are winning,
BY THREE TO NIL!!

↓

48m: HAVERTZ SCORES FOR CHELSEA (3-1)

What a game,
It's safe to say.
It won't be last,
On Match of the Day.

↓

62m: CHELSEA THREATENING

A goal now for Chelsea,
Wouldn't be fun.
I'd get a racing heart,
And a squeaky bum.

↓

93m: IT'S FOUR!!! (4-1)

Enciso shoots,
Mendy saves.
Then Gross gives Roberto,
The win that he craves!!!!!

↓

90+6m: FINAL WHISTLE

In front of De Zerbi,
Potter bowed, then kneeled.
What a result!!
THE WOUND IS HEALED!!

Post-Match Ryhme

The most anticipated match of the season,
Ends with a Roberto win.
Did you see him celebrate?
And did you see his grin?

Potter returned with our ex-backroom staff,
Three points they did seek.
Instead, they left with the north stand chanting,
"Can we play you every week?"

MATCH #14

Saturday, 5 November 2022

Wolverhampton Wanderers 2 – 3 Brighton & Hove Albion

Competition: **Premier League**
Kick-off: **15.00**
Venue: **Molineux Stadium, Wolverhampton**
Weather: **13c, bright**
Referee: **Graham Scott**
Attendance: **30,732**

Squads

Wolves: Sa, Semedo, Collins, Kilman, Bueno, B Traore (Ronan 90), Moutinho, Neves, Podence (Jonny 46), Guedes (Ait-Nouri 74), Hwang (A Traore 68). **Unused subs:** Sarkic, Mosquera, Hodge, Fraser, Griffiths.

Albion: Sanchez, Gross, Dunk, Webster, Estupinan (Gilmour 82), Caicedo, Mac Allister, March, Lallana (Welbeck 65), Mitoma (Veltman 90), Trossard (Undav 82). **Unused subs:** Steele, Lamptey, Colwill, Sarmiento, Enciso.

Match Preview

Our trip to Molineux represented our penultimate Premier League match ahead of the forthcoming FIFA World Cup in Qatar, and we entered it with every reason to be confident.

Our win against Chelsea last time out seemed to have unleashed a wave of optimism within the club's supporters as we finally claimed a win with the dynamic and attack-minded football we'd adopted under Roberto De Zerbi. The 4-1 rout over Graham Potter's side was the first victory in six for De Zerbi, and left us eighth in the Premier League table with 18 points.

Wolves had endured a difficult start to the new season - Bruno Lage had departed as their head coach after just eight games, with Crewe Alexandra boss Steve Davis taking over on an interim basis. They entered the game second bottom with just two wins.

Having been absent from last week's win at the Amex, De Zerbi confirmed that Danny Welbeck would be back in the squad and that Joel Veltman's fitness would be assessed.

Following our 3-0 win in this fixture last season, Albion were looking to win consecutive away league games against Wolves for the first time since winning on our first six visits to Molineux between 1979 and 1991.

Just as we kicked-off, we went under a tornado watch in Oklahoma, so I enjoyed the match with one eye on the TV and the other on the weather app.

AstroPay
AstroPa
10
36

AstroPay
AMERICAN EXPRESS
7
6

13
5

Pre-Match Ryhme

There are 15 minutes 'til kick-off,
It's time to put on a show.
I can't get last week out of my head,
Still basking in the afterglow.

I'm going to make a prediction,
As for goals, we'll score three.
Let's forget that we're playing Wolves,
And pretend they are Chelsea.

In-Match Rhymes

1m: KICK-OFF

Here we go,
A slightly unusual sight.
We're playing away,
But in blue & white.

↓

9m: SOLLY WITH A GREAT CHANCE

Dunk's long ball to Lallana,
That was a great first touch.
Solly's shot deflects wide,
But only just.

↓

10m: GOAL FROM LALLANA!!! [0-1]

Mitoma's right-foot flick,
Across to Leo.
First time to Adam,
Wow, what a trio!

↓

12m: WOLVES RESPOND [1-1]

We've dominated,
Every minute.
A goal from nowhere,
Wolves back in it.

↓

23m: CLOSE FROM LEO

A flowing move,
From our side.
But Leo's left foot,
Sends it high & wide.

34m: VAR AWARDS A PEN TO WOLVES

A Dunk handball?
Proof is elusive.
In my opinion, the replay,
Is inconclusive.

↓

35m: NEVES SCORES [2-1]

I have a scowl,
I have a frown.
And no idea how,
But we're 2-1 down.

↓

44m: KAORU HEADS US LEVEL! [2-2]

A man-of-the-match,
Early contender?
Mitoma's set up by Lallana,
Jinks past defenders.

↓

45+5m: WOLVES DOWN TO 10 MEN

Mitoma through,
The tackle's ugly.
Wolves defender thinking,
He was playing rugby.

↓

HALF-TIME RHYME

We'll know at the final whistle,
If this prediction is true,
But I think we'll come back to win,
By three goals to two.

49m: CLOSE FROM SOLLY!

Mistake at the back,
March makes haste.
Could have squared it to Leo,
Bit of a waste.

↓

67m: MAC ALLISTER DENIED

Free-kick given
22 yards out.
Superb left-foot strike,
Decent shout.

↓

80m: SANCHEZ SAVES

Wolves take,
A short free kick.
Rob gives Lewis,
A bit of stick.

↓

83m: GOAAAL!!! PASCAAALL!! [2-3]

In the second-half,
We've looked a threat.
Now Pascal delivers,
ROOF OF THE NET!

↓

90+5m: FINAL WHISTLE

Whilst my half-time rhyme,
Was typed with conviction.
I now wish I'd put money,
On my prediction.

Post-Match Ryhme

Tonight I'm sitting on the sofa,
As with Mrs Bard I'm staying in.
And on my old and slightly haggard face,
I'm wearing a massive cheesy grin.

We've been waiting for a victory,
Some supporters had begun to cuss.
Then two come along at once,
Just like a London bus.

MATCH #15

Wednesday, 9 November 2022

Arsenal 1 – 3 Brighton & Hove Albion

Competition: **The Carabao Cup – third round**
Kick-off: **19.45**
Venue: **The Emirates Stadium, London**
Weather: **11c, clear**
Referee: **Jarred Gillett**
Attendance: **59,233**

Squads

Arsenal: Hein, Cedric, Holding, Saliba (Gabriel 62), Tierney (Jesus 72), Lokonga (Xhaka 80), Elneny, Nelson, Vieira (Zinchenko 72), Marquinhos (Martinelli), Nketiah. **Unused subs:** Turner, White, Thomas, M. Ødegaard.

Albion: Steele, Lamptey, Veltman, Dunk (Webster 60), Colwill, March (Mitoma 45), Caicedo (Gross 45), Gilmour, Sarmiento (Undav 80), Enciso (Estupinan 76), Welbeck. **Unused subs:** Sanchez, Ferguson, Turns, Moran.

Match Preview

The draw for the third round of the League Cup had been made shortly after our 3-0 away win against Forest Green Rovers in August, and anticipation was high for this all-Premier League clash.

So much had happened since that late August evening in Gloucestershire. Still, with two consecutive wins under our belt, there was a palpable feel-good factor around the club as we headed to the Emirates Stadium.

We had won two of our last three away games against Arsenal; the start of a run that saw Albion finish ninth in the previous season began at Arsenal in April. Having lost six consecutive games, we bounced back with a superb 2-1 victory at the Emirates when Moises Caicedo's made his first Premier League start.

Whilst there were no fresh injury concerns, it was expected Roberto De Zerbi would make numerous changes from the side that won at Wolves last time out, including replacing Rob Sanchez with Jason Steele in goal.

Arsenal were entering their third full season under head coach Mikel Arteta and boasted a record that had seen them progress from 18 of their last 19 League Cup third round ties. They had also won every game they had played at the Emirates in the season so far, so it was likely to be a tough night.

The Albion away support were in full voice as usual, for this cracker of a match.

25
AMERICAN EXPRESS
19
24
34
AMERICAN EXPRESS

2
AMERICAN EXPRESS
22
1 3
70:58
GILMOUR
27
19
20

Pre-Match Ryhme

Ok, here we go,
This afternoon, work I'm shirking.
If you're heading to the Emirates,
I hope the trains are working.

It's the League Cup under lights,
It should be a decent clash.
15 to go, and I'm still not home,
Excuse me, I've got to dash.

In-Match Rhymes

0m: CONGRATULATIONS

So pleased for Levi,
Billy too.
Good luck, lads,
Starting debut.

↓

1m: KICK-OFF

Perfect pitch,
Perfect night.
Red vs. blue,
What a sight.

↓

3m: EARLY CHANCE FOR WELBECK

Sarmineto forward,
Decent play.
But the defender ends up,
Getting in the way.

↓

4m: ENCISO HEADS WIDE

Resulting corner,
Arsenal don't clear.
Julio, from three yards,
Dear, oh dear.

↓

16m: TWO CLOSE LONG-RANGE EFFORTS

Sarmiento first,
Then Julio.
Promising youngsters,
These two, you know.

20m: NKETIAH PUTS ARSENAL IN FRONT (1-0)

Arsenal score,
De Zerbi scowls.
In the build-up,
Sarmiento surely fouled?

↓

26m: PENALTY TO ALBION

Danny through,
Keeper slipped.
Then is flailing arm,
Danny clipped.

↓

27m: EQUALISER!! (1-1)

Danny Welbeck,
Right-foot strike.
Side-footed,
Calm as you like.

↓

42m: JOEL IN THE RIGHT PLACE

Veltman's just brilliant,
So hardworking.
His header clears,
With Nketiah lurking.

↓

HALF-TIME RHYME

One, one,
Seems fair.
Half-time,
All square.

49m: HUGE SAVE FROM STEELE

"To Jason Steele",
Let's raise a toast,
Touches Nketiah's fierce shot,
Onto the post.

↓

58m: BRILLIANT GOAL FROM MITOMA!! (1-2)

A sensational move,
Just world-class,
What a finish,
What a pass!!!!

↓

71m: LAMPTEY SCORES! (1-3)

Can't believe my eyes,
But it is true.
Bloody hell,
I THINK WE'RE GOING THROUGH!

↓

78m: IT'S HAPPENING

Oh dear, Arsenal,
I hope it occurs.
As of right now,
You're heading out with Spurs.

↓

90+5m: FINAL WHISTLE

A perfect display,
Be in no doubt.
We've just knocked,
The league leaders out!

Post-Match Ryhme

Tonight, there are many proud seagulls,
On this side of the pond.
Watching a certain team from Sussex,
Of which we're rather fond.

A great result, well played, lads,
Especially impressive at their place.
Great to see Tariq in full flow,
Man, that lad has got some pace!

MATCH #16

Sunday, 13 November 2022

Brighton & Hove Albion 1 – 2 Aston Villa

Competition: **Premier League**
Kick-off: **14.00**
Venue: **The Amex Stadium, Brighton**
Weather: **15c, sunny**
Referee: **Chris Kavanagh**
Attendance: **31,581**

Squads

Albion: Sanchez, Gross, Dunk, Colwill, Estupinan (Lamptey 80), Caicedo, Mac Allister, March, Lallana (Enciso 4 (Veltman 58)), Trossard, Welbeck (Undav 58). **Unused subs:** Steele, Gilmour, Ferguson, van Hecke, Turns.

Aston Villa: Martínez, Cash, Konsa, Digne (Augustinsson 82'), Mings, Kamara, Douglas Luiz (Dendoncker 83'), Ramsey (Young 69'), McGinn, Buendía (Bailey 74'), Ings (Archer 83'). **Unused subs:** Bednarek, Bailey, Young, Chambers, Archer, Olsen, Sanson, Dendoncker, Augustinsson.

Match Preview

Buoyed by our mid-week defeat of Arsenal four days earlier, a full house at the Amex was hoping for a third consecutive Premier League victory and fourth in all competitions.

Having gone five games without a win under Roberto De Zerbi, we had now enjoyed victories over Chelsea and Wolves in the Premier League before Wednesday night's 3-1 Carabao Cup triumph. We headed into the final round of fixtures before the World Cup break in sixth place with 21 points, knowing that three points could take us to fifth.

After managing only two wins in their opening 11 league games, Aston Villa had recently replaced head coach Steven Gerrard with former Arsenal and Villareal boss Unai Emery who, in turn, had got his reign off to a perfect start the previous Sunday with a 3-1 victory against Manchester United.

Our head coach confirmed he had no fresh injury concerns in his press conference on the Friday afternoon. "Our focus is on Aston Villa," De Zerbi said. "We want to win the game, it's going to be difficult, but we have the potential to win because we're in a good moment. Aston Villa won against United last Sunday, and I watched the game. They have good players."

It turned out to be a frustrating afternoon at the Amex.

Sun Harvest
WOODHART GROUP
mexmast
sales / hire / training / service
AMERICAN EXPRESS
McGINN
7
10

AMERICAN EXPRESS
CAZOO
CAZOO
Search. Drive. Smile.
AMERICAN EXPRESS

Pre-Match Ryhme

It is due to be 15 and sunny,
And not one cloud in the sky.
And I predict shortly after kick-off,
That the high press we'll apply.

I know this may sound boring,
But today, I can't take no five-goal thriller.
I'd be more than happy with a simple one to nil,
Just as long as we beat the Villa.

In-Match Rhymes

1m: KICK-OFF

Just like you,
I've got some sun,
But the difference here is,
That it's minus one!!

↓

1m: WE'RE AHEAD!!! (1-0)

What's going on?
Alexis scores.
We're one-nil up,
Early doors!!

↓

2m: EARLY GOALS

Last time at home,
It was in the fifth minute.
This week it's the first,
Villa defenders complicit.

↓

5m: OH, ADAM

Injuries have been,
His Achilles heel.
Lallana can't continue,
How must he feel?

↓

19m: PENALTY TO VILLA

Should it have been given?
Never, ever.
McGinn falls over Dunk's leg,
Very clever.

20m: VILLA EQUALISE (1-1)

Our complaints,
The ref dismissed.
Ings fires it down the middle,
It nearly broke Rob's wrist.

↓

32m: MARCH NEARLY SCORES FROM A CORNER

It seems many players,
Are trying this now.
Martinez keeps it out,
But I don't quite know how.

↓

HALF-TIME RHYME

I feel a few more chances,
We could have exploited.
After another early goal,
We've looked a bit disjointed.

↓

54m: INGS PUTS VILLA IN FRONT (1-2)

A few seconds after,
They hit the post,
Alexis gets caught,
And the lead they boast.

↓

65m: WHAT A PASS!

Oh my, Colwill,
That's a thing of beauty.
Although Pervis looked offside,
Lino, off duty.

70m: EMBARRASSING FROM VILLA

Conning the ref,
By deceit.
Fall over; hold your head.
And repeat.

↓

71m: HOW ON EARTH?!!!

How is that,
Not a pen, I beg?
Digne has clearly kicked,
Solly's standing leg!!!

↓

80m: DECENT EFFORT BY TROSSARD

A long-range shot by Leo,
Martinez saves.
Then feigns injury,
Our fans rage.

↓

88m: GLORIOUS CHANCE FOR COLWILL!

"We are level",
Was my shout.
But Levi heads over,
From just six yards out.

↓

90+8m: FINAL WHISTLE

The head injury rule,
Has been abused.
Time after time,
It can't be excused.

Post-Match Ryhme

Many years ago I had a soft spot for the Villa,
As the first top-flight game I ever saw,
Was at Villa Park in 1981,
When one-all was the score.

But today, they were so frustrating,
With their annoying time-wasting tricks.
All ten outfield players seemed to be involved,
As well as that bloody guy between the sticks.

MATCH #17

Wednesday, 21 December 2022

Charlton Athletic 0 – 0 Brighton & Hove Albion AET (Charlton win 4-3 on penalties.)

Competition: **The Carabao Cup – fourth round**
Kick-off: **19.45**
Venue: **The Valley, Charlton**
Weather: **9c, overcast**
Referee: **Thomas Bramall**
Attendance: **17,464**

Squads

Charlton: Maynard-Brewer; Inniss, Lavelle, Ness; Chin, Dobson (c), Fraser (Forster-Caskey 75), Sessegnon; Rak-Sakyi, Leaburn (Aneke 63, Stockley 67), Payne (Blackett-Taylor 63). **Unused subs:** MacGillivray, Mitchell, Morgan, Kirk, Campbell.

Albion: Steele, Lamptey, Dunk, Colwill, Gross, March, Lallana (Trossard 62), Enciso (Mitoma 45), Undav (Ferguson 78), Caicedo, Gilmour (Estupinan 62). **Unused subs:** McGill, Sarmiento, Veltman, Moran.

Match Preview

Finally, following a six-week break for the World Cup, Albion returned to action at the Valley against League One opposition in this fourth-round Carabao Cup tie.

The squad had enjoyed some warm-weather training in Dubai in the previous ten days as the club took advantage of the fact that quite a few squad members were already in the Middle East.

We'd reached this stage of the competition thanks to a 3-0 win over Forest Green Rovers and an especially memorable 3-1 victory over Arsenal at the Emirates, whilst the Addicks had beaten QPR, Walsall and Stevenage to get to the fourth round.

With Danny Welbeck and Adam Webster ruled out and Alexis Mac Allister enjoying a break following Argentina's World Cup success, Roberto De Zerbi had indicated that he was keen to give players who hadn't featured as regularly this season, such as Billy Gilmour, Julio Enciso, Levi Colwill & Deniz Undav, an opportunity.

Charlton entered the match on the back of three successive defeats and having just appointed ex-Bristol City boss Dean Holden as their new manager. Holden, however, would be watching from the stands as caretaker manager Anthony Hayes was still in charge for this one.

With the winner of the match earning a place in the quarter-finals, it was a big game to return to.

And we paid the penalty.

RSK
AMERICAN EXPRESS

AMERICAN EXPRESS
AMERICAN EXPRESS
RSK
AMERICAN EXPRESS
CHARLTON
RSK

Pre-Match Ryhme

Can you believe that it's five and a half weeks,
Since we played the Villa?
The World Cup is over, and in our squad,
We now have a World Cup winner.

But Alexis, he won't play today,
As after his World Cup success, he,
Is celebrating hard with the Argentinian team,
Including a certain Lionel Messi.

In-Match Rhymes

1m: KICK-OFF

Come on, lads,
Back to work.
Charlton in red,
We're in hyper turq.

↓

16m: LALLANA HITS THE CROSSBAR

Lamptey doing well,
On the right.
Almost a great start,
To the night.

↓

18m: THEIR KEEPER TIPS OVER

Solly's cross,
Towards the goal, deflected.
Out for a corner,
The ball directed

↓

24m: CHANCE FOR CHARLTON

Payne creates some room,
The chance is real.
But his right-foot shot,
Is straight at Steele.

↓

30m: BOBBLY PITCH

The playing surface,
I don't like.
More undulations,
Than Devil's Dyke.

39m: TREMENDOUS TACKLE FROM DUNK

Oh, our captain,
From a different planet.
Stretched out a leg,
Like Inspector Gadget.

↓

41m: COLWILL DENIED

We're playing well,
I'd say in control.
Levi inches away,
From a debut goal.

↓

HALF-TIME RHYME

Hopefully, in the second half,
A chance we'll take.
But we remain goalless,
At the break.

↓

53m: PENALTY SHOUT FOR ALBION

How's that not given?
Utterly bizarre,
Mitoma gets hacked,
But there's no VAR.

↓

59m: COLWILL CLOSE WITH A HEADER

A Gross free-kick,
Levi rises.
Maynard-Brewer tips it over,
No surprises.

61m: HOW HAS SOLLY MISSED THAT???

Danced past three defenders,
"Goal", I cried,
But after a brilliant run,
He puts it wide.

↓

79m: TROSSARD GOES CLOSE AGAIN

Leo, with his left,
It was going in.
Keeper saves,
He scores, we win. (imo)

↓

80m: FERGUSON SO CLOSE

Mitoma to Pervis,
Left-foot cross,
How we're not ahead,
I'm at a loss.

↓

86m: ANOTHER CHANCE GOES BEGGING

I'm beginning to fear,
We may pay the price.
As it's turning into,
"One of those nights".

↓

90+7m: FINAL WHISTLE

It went to pens,
Neither side did well.
We're heading out,
Oh, bloody hell.

Post-Match Ryhme

You can't expect to win a penalty shoot-out,
If your first two don't go in.
But then again, we should have won in 90,
Where do I begin?

The cobwebs are gone, so better next time,
Is all that we can pray.
The calendar is packed, and next up,
Is Southampton on Boxing Day.

MATCH #18

Monday, 26 December 2022

Southampton 1 – 3 Brighton & Hove Albion

Competition: **Premier League**
Kick-off: **15.00**
Venue: **St. Mary's Stadium, Southampton**
Weather: **9c, bright**
Referee: **Robert Jones**
Attendance: **31,010**

Squads

Southampton: Bazunu, Walker-Peters, Lyanco, Salisu, Perraud (Maitland-Niles 54), Ward-Prowse (S Armstrong 45), Djenepo (Ariboat 45), Elyounoussi (Maraat 78), Edozie (A Armstrong 84), Adams. **Unused subs:** Caleta-Car, Caballero, Bella-Kotchap.

Albion: Sanchez, Veltman, Dunk, Colwill, Estupinan, March (Lamptey 83), Caicedo, Gross (Gilmour 90+1), Mitoma, Lallana (Sarmiento 67), Trossard (Ferguson 83). **Unused subs:** Steele, Enciso, Undav, van Hecke, Moran.

Match Preview

Our first Premier League match following the World Cup saw us head westwards along the south coast to St. Mary's for this Boxing Day clash.

We resumed our top-flight campaign in seventh place, one above Chelsea on goal difference and with 21 points. Our focus was now on making it three Premier League wins from our last four outings, having beaten Chelsea and Wolves in consecutive outings before the home defeat to Aston Villa in November.

We'd also enjoyed relative success on the road, taking ten points from seven away games, while second-bottom Saints had only enjoyed one win at St Mary's this season.

The tie represented the first home game for the newly appointed Southampton manager Nathan Jones. The Welshman was a part of the Albion team that won back-to-back promotions from League Two to the Championship in the early 2000s, before returning as a coach in 2013.

In addition to Alexis Mac Allister, who was still on post-World Cup leave, De Zerbi had confirmed we'd also be without Danny Welbeck and Adam Webster.

For those who made the trip, it was a great Christmas present.

27 28 29
Sportsbet.io
Sportsbet.io
PERRAUD
15
AMERICAN EXPRESS
22
Sportsbet.io
19
AMERICAN EXPRESS
30

AMERICAN EXPRESS
27
AMERICAN EXPRESS
24
MITOMA
22
AMERICAN EXPRESS
6
7
13

Pre-Match Ryhme

Finally, we have got a Premier League game,
It feels like it's been quite a while.
Feels good to be back, and now the aim is,
To return with flair and style.

Last time out, it didn't go so well,
But our Premier League record here hardly varies.
As whilst we've played five games, the omens are good,
As we've yet to lose here at St. Mary's

In-Match Rhymes

0m: A MINUTE'S APPLAUSE

George Cohen departs,
His name in history is fixed.
Only two heroes now left,
From '66.

↓

1m: KICK-OFF

Away the cobwebs,
It's time to blow,
3pm, Boxing Day,
Here we go!

↓

3m: MAGIC FEET FROM MITOMA

It's sensational skill,
I'm in awe.
Beautiful dribbling,
But couldn't score.

↓

14m: LALLANA NODS US AHEAD!!!! (0-1)

Solly's cross,
Off Adam's head, it flew,
And goes straight through the fingers,
Of Bazunu!!

↓

22m: ALBION DOMINANT

Every player,
Putting in a session.
Away from home,
And 80% possession.

26m: SOUTHAMPTON CLOSE WITH A FREE-KICK

On the fact he'd score,
Some would have bet their house.
But luckily, it flies just wide,
From James Ward-Prouse.

↓

35m: SOUTHAMPTON OWN GOAL! (0-2)

Pervis is an early,
Man of the match contender.
His cross for Solly,
Goes in off the defender,

↓

39m: CHANCE FOR KAORU

Pervis to Leo,
Leo to Mitoma.
But our Japanese international,
Heads just over.

↓

HALF-TIME RHYME

We're back in business,
It seems to me.
Ahead by two,
But hope it will soon be three.

↓

48m: LET-OFF FOR ALBION

My prediction,
About being up by three,
Looks a bit premature,
A huge chance for Edozie.

56m: SENSATIONAL SOLLY!! (0-3)

Solly cuts in,
25-yard left-foot strike.
I think Johnny Cantor,
Has just broken his mic!!!

↓

60m: OH, KAURO!!

A super cross from Solly,
How did we not score?
Simple header for Mitoma,
Should have been four.

↓

71m: PENALTY TO SOUTHAMPTON

Edozie runs into Gross,
But I'd like to know,
Where is Pascal,
Supposed to go?

↓

73m: SANCHEZ SAVES, REBOUND PUT AWAY (1-3)

Unlucky Rob,
Decent save.
Pen in the first place?
Oh, behave.

↓

90+5m: FINAL WHISTLE

Christmas celebration?
Here's a reason.
Our fourth away win,
Of the season!

Post-Match Ryhme

We should remember our players are human,
And they all have their ups and downs.
Such a shame they have to put up with,
Too many anonymous online clowns.

De Zerbi's put his arm around Solly,
In the lad, what faith he's shown.
That's now been repaid - what a strike!!
Undoubtedly one of our own.

MATCH #19

Saturday, 31 December 2022

Brighton & Hove Albion 2 – 4 Arsenal

Competition: **Premier League**
Kick-off: **17.30**
Venue: **The Amex Stadium, Brighton**
Weather: **13c, damp.**
Referee: **Anthony Taylor**
Attendance: **31,647**

Squads

Albion: Sanchez, Lamptey, Dunk, Colwill, Estupinan, Gilmour, Lallana (Sarmiento 59), March (Enciso 76), Gross, Mitoma, Trossard (Ferguson 59). **Unused subs:** Steele, van Hecke, Veltman, Turns, Moran, Hinshelwood.

Arsenal: Ramsdale, White (Tomiyasu 60), Saliba, Gabriel, Zinchenko (Tierney 60), Ødegaard (Holding 87), Partey (Elneny 74), Xhaka, Saka, Nketiah, Martinelli. **Unused subs:** Soares, Vieira, Lokonga, Marquinhos, Turner.

Match Preview

We said farewell to 2022 with a late Saturday afternoon kick-off at the Amex as we attempted to repeat our League Cup exploits of early November in north London.

Both sides went into the game on the back of 3-1 wins on Boxing Day. An own goal plus strikes from Adam Lallana and Solly March had secured three points at Southampton, whilst Arsenal had a five-point lead at the top of the table after their win against West Ham at the Emirates.

Albion had one change enforced, with Moises Caicedo suspended after collecting his fifth booking of the season at St Mary's. De Zerbi also confirmed that we would be without Adam Webster and Danny for the second weekend.

Albion had an impressive recent record against the Gunners. We were aiming for our third successive win against them, having beaten them 3-1 the previous month in the Carabao Cup and 2-1 when we met them in the league at the Emirates in April with Leandro Trossard and Enock Mwepu on the score sheet.

In the press conference a day earlier, head coach Roberto De Zerbi had said: "At the moment, the players are in good condition. Adam Webster and Danny Welbeck aren't able to play, and we will have to wait a few more days for Welbeck, maybe a bit longer for Webster.

Unfortunately, however, Arsenal were intent on revenge.

sky
UNIBET
AMERICAN EXPRESS

13
GABRIEL
6
GILMOUR
27
AMERICAN EXPRESS

Pre-Match Ryhme

I can't wait until tomorrow,
It's the last game of the year.
They may be top of the table,
But of Arsenal, we hold no fear.

It's a shame that we won't have Moises,
So young but so mature.
But it also presents an opportunity,
The stage is yours, Billy Gilmour.

In-Match Rhymes

1m: KICK-OFF

Damp conditions,
Under the lights.
Arsenal in black,
Us blue & white.

↓

2m: WE'RE BEHIND (0-1)

In possession,
Lamptey caught.
Saka scores,
Who'd have thought?

↓

4m: VITAL SAVE FROM ROB

Frantic opening,
Constant pressure.
Zinchenko through,
Arsenal the aggressor.

↓

16m: GREAT ALBION MOVE

We're creating chances,
Leo denied,
As Ramsdale manages,
To tip it wide.

↓

18m: SALIBA CLEARS OFF THE LINE

A corner from Gross,
It almost crosses the line.
We needed some intervention,
From the divine.

39m: ODEGAARD ADDS A SECOND (0-2)

Cleared from a corner,
Oh, that was tough.
It wasn't a perfect contact,
But it was enough.

↓

HALF-TIME RHYME

They're ahead,
Fair play.
Probably deserved,
I have to say.

↓

47m: NKETIAH WITH A THIRD (0-3)

I heard someone had scored,
But was in the kitchen and when,
I came back in, I saw,
That it was not us but them.

↓

65m: MMITTTOOMMMAAAA!!! (1-3)

Pascal to Kaoru,
Then back of the net.
Come on now, lads,
There's life in this yet!

↓

71m: MARTINELLI MAKES IT FOUR (1-4)

I understand,
If you choose to lampoon,
"There's life in this yet"?
Seems I spoke too soon.

77m: FERGUSON'S FIRST PL GOAL!!! (2-4)

Celebrations after scoring,
He quickly forgot.
Instead, Evan puts the ball,
Back on the centre spot.

↓

89m: MITOMA...ALMOST!!

Mitoma scores,
We never say die.
VAR says he was offside,
Man, I could cry.

↓

90m: REALLY?!

Kaoru was running away from goal,
The letter of the law applied.
But the studs of his rear boot,
Were the only bit offside.

↓

91m: STILL A CHANCE?

Can we score two,
In added time?
Like Man United
In '99?

↓

90+7m: FINAL WHISTLE

We lose 4-2,
The result was fair.
But imagine us with Moises,
And Mac Allister.

Post-Match Ryhme

I don't think we were quite switched on,
As the game got started.
As a few of our early possessions,
They seemed a bit half-hearted.

But decisions also went against us,
And their fourth went through Rob's legs.
So with just a few hours to go, roll on 2023,
Let's have some better luck, I begs.

MATCH #20

Tuesday, 3 January 2023

Everton 1 – 4 Brighton & Hove Albion

Competition: **Premier League**
Kick-off: **19.45**
Venue: **Goodison Park, Liverpool**
Weather: **13c, raining**
Referee: **Andre Marriner**
Attendance: **39,103**

Squads

Everton: Pickford, Patterson (Coleman 63), Coady, Tarkowski, Mykolenko, Iwobi, Gueye (Maupay 64), Davies (Doucouré 58), McNeil (Price 58), Calvert-Lewin (Simms 83), Gray. **Unused subs:** Mina, Begovic, Godfrey, Vinagre.

Albion: Sanchez, Veltman (Lamptey 70), Dunk, Colwill, Estupinan, March (Moran 78), Gross, Sarmiento (Mac Allister 62), Caicedo, Mitoma (Lallana 78), Ferguson (Enciso 70). **Unused subs:** Steele, Trossard, van Hecke.

Match Preview

Albion kicked off 2023 as they did 2022 with a trip to Goodison Park to face Everton.

We entered the match with an impressive away record this campaign, having won four of our eight games on the road, and, despite suffering a defeat to Arsenal on New Year's Eve, we'd also won three of our last five outings in the league and could move up from ninth to as high as seventh with a win.

Frank Lampard's Everton were in 16th place, a point above the bottom three after they ended a run of three straight league defeats with an excellent 1-1 draw at Manchester City three days earlier. Another boost for the Toffees was striker Dominic Calvert-Lewin's return after injury.

Everton sat in 16th position with 15 points and had only won twice at Goodison this season. The last time was on 22 October when they beat Crystal Palace 3-0.

The big team news was that Alexis Mac Allister was back in contention after returning from his post-World Cup break, and Moises Caicedo was available again after serving a one-match suspension against Arsenal. However, Roberto De Zerbi also confirmed that we would still be without Adam Webster and Danny Welbeck, who had not played for us since the Premier League restarted after the World Cup break.

It was wet and miserable in the northwest.

And raining goals, too.

hummel
BOXT
Stake

Pre-Match Ryhme

The A23 and then the M23,
Are first up if you drive.
Then you take the M40 northwest,
If you get past the M25!

Then probably the M42, the M6,
Then, if I were you,
I'd get off at junction 21a,
And head to Goodison on the M62

In-Match Rhymes

1m: KICK-OFF

We're in crimson,
Lovely sight.
And are playing left,
From the right.

↓

5m: SUPERB SAVE FROM SANCHEZ!

Well done, Rob,
A real test.
Everton claim handball,
Referee unimpressed.

↓

10m: MITOMA HEADS OVER

Just like at Southampton,
A goal looked on.
But after a cross from Solly,
Kaoru gets his angles wrong.

↓

15m: GOAL! THAT'S BETTER, KAORU!!! (0-1)

Great ball from Moises,
To the left wing.
Mitoma cuts inside,
And fires it in!!!

↓

20m: FERGUSON HITS THE POST

In from Mitoma,
Shame it wasn't Solly,
As it would have rhymed,
With "Great left-foot volley".

24m: NOW JUST OVER FROM EVAN!

We break from midfield,
Ferguson has a go.
It flies over,
But not by much, you know.

↓

26m: OUTSTANDING SAVE FROM ROB

He had the confidence,
To come off his line.
He cuts out the cross,
But ends up supine.

↓

HALF-TIME RHYME

Plenty of late pressure,
It must be said.
But at half-time,
We're still one ahead.

↓

52m: FERGUSON DOUBLES OUR LEAD!!! (0-2)

From Sarmiento to Evan,
The ball does reach.
Our young Irishman goalscoring instinct,
You just can't teach.

↓

54m: SOLLY MAKES IT THREE! (0-3)

Everton at the back,
In sixes and sevens,
They're on the floor,
We are in heaven.

57m: GROSS WITH A LOVELY CHIP! (0-4)

"There's only one Der Kaiser",
From the rooftops, shout.
It's Pascal,
And it's a rout!

↓

62m: CHANGE FOR ALBION

The club did a lovely celebration,
To welcome him back.
Our World Cup winner comes on,
Alexis Mac

↓

90+1m: PENALTY TO EVERTON

Rob takes Iwobi out,
Rush of blood to the head.
Obvious pen,
It has to be said.

↓

90+2m: EVERTON SCORE (1-4)

Straight down the middle
From Demarai Gray.
No clean sheet,
For Rob today.

↓

90+4m: FINAL WHISTLE

Oh, the smiles,
The boys can't hide,
Everton swamped,
By a crimson tide.

Post-Match Ryhme

It seems that not too long ago,
We were struggling to score.
But tonight, we went to Goodison,
And won by one to four.

And what about Evan Ferguson?
Yes, his full debut took a while.
But everyone's predicting such a bright future,
For our young lad from the Emerald Isle.

MATCH #21

Saturday, 7 January 2023

Middlesbrough 1 – 5 Brighton & Hove Albion

Competition: **The Emirates FA Cup – third round**
Kick-off: **15.00**
Venue: **The Riverside Stadium, Middlesbrough**
Weather: **11c, partly sunny**
Referee: **Simon Hooper**
Attendance: **21,982**

Squads

Middlesborough: Steffen, Smith, Fry, McNair, Giles (Bola 81), Forss (Watmore 59), Howson, Hackney (Mowatt 59), McGree (Jones 59), Akpom, Crooks (Archer 68). **Unused subs:** Carvalho, Hoppe, Roberts, Gitau.

Albion: Steele, Lamptey, van Hecke, Colwill, Estupinan, March, Gross, Caicedo, Mitoma (Enciso 64), Lallana (Mac Allister 45), Ferguson (Welbeck 64). **Unused subs:** McGill, Webster, Sarmiento, Undav, Gilmour.

Match Preview

We began our journey in the FA Cup by heading north to face Middlesbrough at the Riverside Stadium, hoping to repeat the 2-1 win we enjoyed against West Bromwich Albion at this stage last season.

Last year Boro had reached the quarterfinals, beating Manchester United on penalties before seeing off Spurs in the fifth round. Their fine run was brought to an end by Chelsea, who won 2-0 at the Riverside.

Former Manchester United and England midfielder Michael Carrick had taken over as Boro boss from Chris Wilder in late October and had seen his side embark on a terrific run in the Championship. They had won seven of their last nine league games and had climbed to fifth in the table.

Our last meeting with Boro had also been in the FA Cup when, five years earlier, Glenn Murray had fired home in the 90th minute to secure a 1-0 victory in a fourth round tie. Interestingly, of the squad used that day, only Lewis Dunk and Pascal Gross were still at the club.

De Zerbi had referenced the League Cup loss to Charlton when hinting he would name a strong squad and that it would feature the returning Danny Welbeck and Deniz Undav.

Tough game on paper. But we delivered.

UNIBET
MITOMA
22
AMERICAN EXPRESS
32Red

Pre-Match Ryhme

We are the boys & girls from Sussex,
That's Sussex by the Sea.
And we're heading to the Riverside,
With thoughts of Wembley.

But Middleborough are in decent form,
Which seems to have coincided,
With Carrick arriving, they're suddenly thriving,
Over a renaissance, he has presided.

In-Match Rhymes

1m: KICK-OFF

Not a full house,
It would appear.
But still a cracking,
Atmosphere.

↓

8m: WE'RE AHEAD!!!!! (0-1)

Our fans go ballistic,
What a sound!!!
Solly's shot saved,
Gross on the rebound!

↓

11m: LALLANA DENIED

I'm sure their side,
Has a younger demographic.
But right now,
It's one-way traffic.

↓

13m: THE HOSTS HIT BACK (1-1)

From an Akpom header,
The ball squirms.
Over the line,
Back on level terms.

↓

22m: JASON STEELE

Route one from Boro,
Saved by the former.
Tipped it over,
The result's a corner.

30m: LALLANA!!!!!! (1-2)

It was going in from Mitoma,
I suggest.
But Adam makes sure,
In off his chest!!!

↓

38m: NAUGHTY MITOMA?

In their area,
Kauro goes down.
Was there contact?
If not, I frown.

↓

40m: GOOD OR BAD?

Let's hope this fact,
The game won't mar.
But a reminder today,
We've no VAR.

↓

HALF-TIME RHYME

In the last 15 minutes,
Far less action.
But at half-time,
Huge satisfaction.

↓

58m: OH, ALEXIS! GOAL! (1-3)

I missed it at first,
As it happened so fast.
What a cheeky flick!!
World Cup winning class!!!

71m: TWO FREE-KICKS

Both from Alexis,
Both goals, almost.
One flies just wide,
One hits the post.

↓

79m: ALEXIS COMPLETES HIS BRACE!!!! (1-4)

He picked his spot,
In it went!!!
I have to say,
Their defence looks spent.

↓

87m: HE NEEDED THAT (1-5)

He has been struggling,
A little bit.
Deniz Undav!
Lovely hit!!

↓

90m: WE CAN'T FINISH?

Imagine a few months ago,
If you, I'd told,
We'd score nine in two.
I'd be getting trolled!!

↓

90+2m: FINAL WHISTLE

Boro's Cup dreams,
Go up in flames.
Whilst we've scored 12,
In our last three away games.

Post-Match Ryhme

It was clear Roberto wasn't happy,
When we lost to Charlton in the Cup.
I speculate these were his thoughts,
When that night a glass of Chianti he did sup.

"I want to win some silverwear,
So, no one be in any doubt.
When we play in the third round of the FA Cup,
I'm putting my very best side out!"

MATCH #22

Saturday, 14 January 2023

Brighton & Hove Albion 3 – 0 Liverpool

Competition: **Premier League**
Kick-off: **15.00**
Venue: **The Amex Stadium, Brighton**
Weather: **12c, dull**
Referee: **Darren England**
Attendance: **31,645**

Squads

Albion: Sanchez, Dunk (Webster 90), Colwill, Estupinan, March, Gross, Caicedo, Mitoma (Lamptey 90), Mac Allister (Sarmiento 83), Lallana (Veltman 65), Ferguson (Welbeck 65). **Unused subs:** Steele, Undav, Gilmour, van Hecke.

Liverpool: Alisson, Alexander-Arnold, Matip (Gomez, 69), Konate, Robertson, Fabinho (Keita, 69), Thiago, Henderson (Elliott, 69), Oxlade-Chamberlain (Doak, 69), Salah, Gakpo. **Unused subs:** Kelleher, Milner, Jones, Tsimikas, Carvalho.

Match Preview

We returned to Premier League action 10 days after beating Everton by taking on their bitter rivals at the Amex.

Overall we'd been in excellent form — winning four of our last six league games — but De Zerbi would have undoubtedly been looking for an improvement in our home form as we had picked up just four points from his five matches at the Amex.

Sitting in eighth place, we'd played all seven teams above us in the table once and picked up five points from those games. One of those came at Anfield in October when Roberto was in the Albion dugout for the first time, and we secured a point in an enthralling 3-3 draw thanks to a Leandro Trossard hat-trick.

Going into the game, Liverpool were a point better off than us, and Jurgen Klopp's men knew that victory would move them to within four points of the Champions League places.

On the other hand, three points for us would mean we'd have beaten Liverpool at home for the first time in the Premier League and would see us move above them into seventh - a point behind sixth-placed Fulham.

Our head coach had indicated there were no new injury concerns and that he had a full squad to choose from. Leandro Trossard was not involved after speculation about his future.

Not a bad one, this one!

THIAGO
standard chartered
apollo

Pre-Match Ryhme

I'm writing this in Florida,
As I get some winter sun.
And celebrate my birthday,
I can't believe I'm still 21.

I'm watching in a crowded sports bar,
In Daytona Beach.
Come on, boys, it's a huge game,
Three points, please, I beseech.

In-Match Rhymes

1m: KICK-OFF

Looking forward to this one,
I have to say.
Liverpool get us,
Underway.

↓

4m: EARLY FREE-KICK DISCUSSIONS

Alexis smiled at Gross,
And just said "bro",
"I get lots of chances,
You have a go!"

↓

8m: MARCH'S SHOT CLEARED OFF THE LINE

Sweeping move,
Solly denied.
Although I think his shot,
Was heading wide.

↓

10m: I AGREE

The club's admin,
Is indicating,
That our play,
Is scintillating!

↓

12m: WE'RE DOMINATING

Have to say,
On the whole,
There's only one side in it,
We're in control.

29m: WIDE FROM KAORU

Great ball from Colwill,
Mitoma just onside.
Shoots with his right foot,
Ball goes just wide.

↓

41m: PENALTY REVOKED FOR OFFSIDE

Alisson brings down Solly,
Penalty shout.
Ref goes ahead and gives it,
Then rules it out.

↓

45+1m: EVAN WITH A CHANCE

Unselfish from Solly,
After a great attack,
Ferguson can't generate power,
As he's leaning back.

↓

HALF-TIME RHYME

So fast when he's sprinting,
Mitoma looks blurred.
We just need to be more clinician,
In our final third.

↓

47m: GOALLLL!! WE'RE AHEAD!! (1-0)

Liverpool mistake,
As they dropped deeper.
Solly flicks it under,
Their outrushing keeper!!!!

53m: WOW!! GREAT STRIKE FROM SOLLY!! (2-0)

He managed to dig it out,
From under his feet.
Sensational, Solly!!!
His brace is complete.

↓

63m: ALBION CRUISING

If our team were a person,
They'd be smiling, I think.
And with a shrug of their shoulders.
They'd give you a wink.

↓

76m: LIVERPOOL CHANCE

The smile on my face.
I'm trying to hide,
As from 12 yards out,
Elliott drags it four yards wide.

↓

82m: DAAAANNNNNNY!!! (3-0)

Brilliant close control,
Over Gomez's head he flicks.
Like Gazza's goal against Scotland,
In Euro '96!!!

↓

90+3m: FINAL WHISTLE

What a performance,
We were ruthless.
As for Liverpool,
They were toothless.

Post-Match Ryhme

That was a truly fantastic performance,
We were a constant threat.
But if you compare the teams, you have to say,
The result's not a huge upset.

For some now, it's passports out,
As we're hoping to go on tour.
And you have to say, although its only January,
Talk of Europe ain't premature.

MATCH #23

Saturday, 21 January 2023

Leicester City 2 – 2 Brighton & Hove Albion

Competition: **Premier League**
Kick-off: **15.00**
Venue: **The King Power Stadium, Leicester**
Weather: **2c, sunny**
Referee: **Thomas Bramall**
Attendance: **32,056**

Squads

Leicester: Ward, Castagne, Amartey, Faes, Thomas, Praet (Albrighton 35), Tielemans, Mendy, Barnes, Vardy (Daka 86), Dewsbury-Hall (Maddison 69). **Unused subs:** Söyüncü, Iheanacho, Vestergaard, Iversen, Brunt, McAteer.

Albion: Sanchez, Dunk, van Hecke (Lamptey 77), Gross, Estupinan, Caicedo, Mac Allister, March, Mitoma, Lallana (Veltman 29), Welbeck (Ferguson 65). **Unused subs:** Steele, Webster, Sarmiento, Enciso, Undav, Gilmour.

Match Preview

The away fixture against Leicester gave us the opportunity to make it three consecutive Premier League wins.

Back-to-back victories over Everton and Liverpool had maintained our place in the top eight, and we were six points better off after 18 games than in any of our previous five Premier League seasons.

We also had five wins from nine on the road so far and the joint fourth-best goal difference in the league.

On the other hand, the Foxes were going through one of their most challenging periods under Brendan Rodgers. Having revived their form in October and November, they had suffered four consecutive league defeats since the World Cup break. In that post-World Cup run, they'd only scored once, although they had faced three teams in the top six — Newcastle, Liverpool and Fulham.

Roberto De Zerbi confirmed that, aside from a 'muscular problem' with Levi Colwill, we had no fresh injury concerns.

The reverse fixture at the Amex had taken place the previous September and had been memorable not only for our 5-2 romp to victory but also for the fact it was Graham Potter's final match in charge.

Could we repeat the feat?

FBS
trade online
AMERICAN EXPRESS
22
CAICEDO
25
9

FBS
AMARTEY
18
28
24

Pre-Match Ryhme

It's the perfect afternoon for football,
OK, perhaps a little cold.
But as the sun hangs low above the King Power,
Allow me to be a little bold.

Whilst it may not be a repeat of September,
When the Foxes, we did trounce.
I'm quietly confident we'll beat them again today,
To make it three wins on the bounce.

In-Match Rhymes

1m: KICK-OFF

Blue v crimson,
Cold, no snow.
Danny kicks off,
Here we go.

↓

2m: OUR BACK FOUR

Gross now at right back,
A little fiddle.
Jan Paul joins Lewis,
In the middle.

↓

14m: PERFECT PERVIS

Leicester break,
Vardy is through.
Who intercepts?
You know who.

↓

24m: CHANCE FOR VAN HECKE

Pascal's corner
Jan Paul back post.
For his first goal,
Almost a toast.

↓

27m: MITOOOMA!! [1-0]

OK, Kaoru,
Drop the mic.
Right foot, top corner,
WHAT A STRIKE!!!!!!!!

38m: ALBRIGHTON EQUALISES [1-1]

Leicester score,
Messy affair.
Half-time looms,
And we're all square.

↓

HALF-TIME RHYME

A difficult game to summarise,
We've done OK.
I think we should be leading,
On the balance of play

↓

51m: PENALTY APPEAL

Danny tripped,
Our pleas overlooked.
Roberto furious,
He gets booked.

↓

57m: MARCH FIRES OVER!

Whilst the build-up from Mitoma,
Was sublime.
On TV, Glenn Murray
Suggests Solly had too much time.

↓

63m: LEICESTER LEAD [2-1]

From a corner,
Luke Thomas flicks it on.
Barnes back post,
Our lead is gone.

76m: WARD DENIES MARCH

Solly is through,
But the keeper's there.
A fierce strike,
Should have played it square?

↓

80m: LAMPTEY WITH A CHANCE

Lovely interplay,
Between Tariq and Gross.
Loops on top of the net,
Not that close.

↓

84m: MAGIC FROM MAC ALLISTER

Our World Cup winner,
To us is key.
His shot is saved,
By the keeper's knee.

↓

88m: EVAN WITH AN EQUALISER!!!!! [2-2]

PANDEMONIUM!!
I'll end this rhyme.
By shouting loudly,
IT'S FERGIE TIME!!!

↓

90+5m: FINAL WHISTLE

Match summary,
In just two verse.
Could have been better,
Could have been worse.

Post-Match Ryhme

I'm not really sure what to feel,
As on another day,
I think we would have claimed all three points,
But it's never easy when you play away.

The King Power Stadium in Leicester,
Although we thrashed them last time out,
Today proves you can never count your chickens,
So maybe a point's a decent shout.

MATCH #24

Sunday, 29 January 2023

Brighton & Hove Albion 2 – 1 Liverpool

Competition: **The FA Cup – fourth round**
Kick-off: **13.30**
Venue: **The Amex Stadium, Brighton**
Weather: **8c, bright**
Referee: **David Coote**
Attendance: **31,675**

Squads

Albion: Steele, Lamptey, Webster (Veltman 45), Dunk, Estupinan, March, Mac Allister, Gross, Mitoma, Welbeck (Gilmour 67), Ferguson (Undav 87). **Unused subs:** Sanchez, Sarmiento, Enciso, van Hecke, Moran, Hinshelwood.

Liverpool: Alisson, Alexander-Arnold (Milner 59), Konaté, Gomez, Robertson, Thiago Alcántara (Jones 79), Bajcetic (Fabinho 85), Keïta (Henderson 59), Salah, Gakpo, Elliott (Núñez 59). **Unused subs:** Oxlade-Chamberlain, Tsimikas, Matip, Kelleher.

Match Preview

So here we were, back at the Amex for a second consecutive home game against Jurgen Klopp's men. It was just a fortnight since our stunning 3-0 win in the Premier League and time to see if we could do it all over again in the FA Cup – and 39 years to the day since we beat Liverpool 2-0 in the competition at the Goldstone.

We'd scored three goals in both of our meetings with Liverpool this season, having done so in just two of our first 35 against the Reds in all competitions and were looking to win consecutive games against Liverpool for the first time in our history.

Whilst we had cruised into the fourth round of the FA Cup with a thumping 5-1 win over Middlesbrough, holders Liverpool had been taken to a replay before beating Wolves 1-0 after the teams drew 2-2 at Anfield.

Roberto De Zerbi had confirmed that Adam Lallana and Levi Colwill would miss the game through injury, but, on a positive note, he was also confident that we could play much better than we had against Leicester last time out.

And he was right.

standard chartered
26
2
18
28
1
10
11
betway

Snickers
JONES
17
standard chartered
close to t
ction
You'
18
21
5
close to the a
re this close

Pre-Match Ryhme

It was only two short weeks ago,
Wow, did we put on a show?!
A 3-0 win against today's opponents,
Now they're back again, although.

They'll be looking for revenge,
But I'm sure I'm the same as you,
In hoping that, in a few hours,
We'll all be experiencing déjà vu.

In-Match Rhymes

1m: KICK-OFF

I can't wait for this one,
I have to say.
As the visitors get us,
Underway.

↓

4m: GOAL-LINE CLEARANCE FROM DUNK!

Salah should score!
On our defence, depending.
First Webster, then Lewis,
Great defending.

↓

15m: GREAT CHANCE FOR FERGUSON!

Gross to Solly,
Down the right wing.
Pulls it back,
Evan's shot lacks sting.

↓

21m: CREATING CHANCES

Mitoma and Evan,
On the left combining.
The former scruffs his shot,
But what a signing.

↓

30m: LIVERPOOL TAKE THE LEAD (0-1)

Elliott onside,
But not by much.
Bottom left-hand corner,
Steele got a touch.

39m: DUNK!! WE'RE LEVEL!!! (1-1)

A short corner cleared,
Tariq hits a ripper.
Which gets a deflection,
Off the skipper!!!

↓

HALF-TIME RHYME

A fifth round place,
Is what's at stake.
It's all square,
At the break.

↓

48m: SOLLY THE PROVIDER

Lovely cross from March,
Aiming for the back post.
Mitoma is enjoying,
Trent on toast.

↓

50m: DUNK'S FREE-KICK JUST WIDE

Our captain taking free kicks?
Some may scoff.
But that's a decent effort,
Not far off.

↓

55m: GROSS HAMMERS OVER

Mitoma skins the defender,
Which isn't surprising.
Results in a volley from Gross,
Which was always rising.

72m: ALISSON SAVES – SOMEHOW!

Mitoma crosses it in,
Outside of the boot.
How Solly hasn't scored,
I can't compute.

↓

80m: CLOSE FROM EVAN

Solly turns provider,
How are we not ahead?
Evan's right foot shot,
Deflected, corner instead.

↓

83m: HOW IS THAT NOT A RED?!!

Evan forced off,
Studs-up tackle with force.
Fabinho rightly showing,
A little remorse.

↓

90+3m: MMIIITTTTOOOOMMMMAAAA!!!! (2-1)

This might be,
His best goal yet!!
What sublime close control,
ROOF OF THE NET!!!!

↓

90+7m: FINAL WHISTLE

It's so clear,
What this win means.
The fifth round beckons,
OH, THE SCENES!!!!!!

Post-Match Ryhme

Liverpool's Bill Shankly,
Once said about this sport,
That it was more important than life or death,
He wasn't right, but here's a thought.

There ARE more important things in life,
But as I see the north stand sing our song,
It reminds us that football gives us something special,
It helps us feel that we 'belong'.

MATCH #25

Saturday, 4 February 2023

Brighton & Hove Albion 1 – 0 AFC Bournemouth

Competition: **Premier League**
Kick-off: **15.00**
Venue: **The Amex Stadium, Brighton**
Weather: **9c, partly sunny**
Referee: **Craig Pawson**
Attendance: **31,600**

Squads

Albion: Sanchez, Lamptey (Buonanotte 75), Veltman, Dunk, Estupinan, Gilmour (Caicedo 57), Gross, March (Webster 89), Mitoma, Undav (Enciso 75), Welbeck (Sarmiento 57). **Unused subs:** Steele, van Hecke, Offiah, Moran.

Bournemouth: Neto; Smith, Mepham, Senesi, Zemura, Lerma, Billing (Rothwell, 66); Ouattara, Traorè (Christie, 61), Anthony (Viña, 85), Semenyo. **Unused subs:** Travers, Stacey, Moore, Pollock, Greenwood, Kinsey-Wellings.

Match Preview

We entered the game against Bournemouth on the back of what had to have been one of our best months in the top-flight.

Four wins and a draw during January, including victories over Liverpool in both the league and the FA Cup, had seen us heading into the match with confidence sky-high.

We sat sixth in the Premier League, five points behind Spurs and with two games in hand, but with only three points between Albion and the five teams below us in the table.

The Cherries had just as great a motive to bag three points. Sat in 18th, a win could catapult them as high as 14th. Gary O'Neil's team had struggled for form since the return to action after the World Cup, picking up one point from five games and scoring once in their draw against Nottingham Forest the previous week.

To arrest that slump, they had been particularly active in the January transfer window, bringing in Dango Ouattara from Lorient, Antoine Semenyo from Bristol City and Illya Zabarnyi from Dynamo Kyiv, as well as goalkeeper Darren Randolph from West Ham.

Roberto De Zerbi had confirmed that Adam Lallana would not be fit in time for the game, joining Levi Colwill and Jakub Moder on the sidelines.

He also indicated that, following the injury picked up against Liverpool the previous weekend, Evan Ferguson was a doubt.

Big game this one. But weren't they all?

dafabet
AMERICAN EXPRESS
21
33
NETO
O.DANGO
11
WELBECK
18
29
6
27
34

Pre-Match Ryhme

On the Great Plains it's 04.30,
And I'm lying in my bed.
And thoughts about the match today,
Seem to be dominating my head.

I'm imagining the scenes in Sussex,
As you all prepare.
Maybe you're in the pub, or on the train,
Oh, I wish I could be there.

In-Match Rhymes

1m: KICK-OFF

Danny gets us,
Underway.
On this cool,
Midwinter's day.

↓

2m: WELBECK IN THE THICK OF IT

He challenged their keeper,
They both connected.
But surely 50/50,
Are keepers too protected?

↓

9m: BIG CHANCE AS DENIZ IS PLAYED IN

Possible penalty?
There were murmurs.
As Deniz turned on,
His afterburners.

↓

13m: THREE CHANCES FOR UNDAV!!

A goal on his full PL debut,
He could almost boast.
First one blocked, second one saved,
Third one hits the post!!

↓

17m: SOMEHOW BOURNEMOUTH FAIL TO SCORE

Numerous chances,
For both sides.
Good move from our opponents,
But Lerma puts it wide.

31m: GILMOUR EFFORT BLOCKED

Billy shoots the ball,
Across terra firma.
But he fires his shot,
Straight at Lerma.

↓

35m: ALBION DENIED

Solly's cross,
Then Mitoma, too.
How we haven't scored,
I have no clue.

↓

40m: WELBECK NODS STRAIGHT AT NETO

Three defenders around him,
As Solly's cross came in.
But none made a challenge,
A defensive sin.

↓

45m: INCHES FROM GOING AHEAD

Deniz pings one in,
On the floor.
Danny couldn't have done,
Any more.

↓

HALF-TIME RHYME

We've had chances,
But so have they.
It could be 3-2,
On another day.

57m: CLOSE FROM GILMOUR

Past the left-hand post,
His shot was clubbed.
Nearly his first goal,
But he's now been subbed.

↓

69m: BRILLIANT DEFENDING

Bournemouth break,
Two on one.
But what a block from Pervis,
Wow, can that lad run!

↓

86m: CLOSE FROM MITOMA

Sarmiento to Kaoru,
Great close control.
Their keeper blocks,
Another chance on goal.

↓

87m: MITOMA HEADS US IN FRONT!!!!! (1-0)

His name is Kaoru,
And he ain't that tall.
But in a crowded box,
HE'S FIRST TO THE BALL!!!!!

↓

90+4m: FINAL WHISTLE

A crucial win,
And three more points.
Our Japanese winger,
Never disappoints.

Post-Match Ryhme

Can you believe it, for the second week,
Mitoma's goal secures the win?
Resulting in a Hoveite in Oklahoma,
Wearing the biggest grin.

When it comes to Europe, that could be huge,
As it's sure to be very tight.
So, I hope you all have a fantastic evening,
And celebrate long into the night.

MATCH #26

Saturday, 11 February 2023

Crystal Palace 1 – 1 Brighton & Hove Albion

Competition: **Premier League**
Kick-off: **15.00**
Venue: **Selhurst Park, London**
Weather: **9c, overcast**
Referee: **Michael Oliver**
Attendance: **24,027**

Squads

Palace: Guaita, Clyne, Tomkins, Guéhi, Mitchell, Doucouré, Hughes (Lokonga 56), Olise (Ahamada 84), Ayew, Schlupp (Eze 71), Mateta (Edouard 71). **Unused subs:** Johnstone, Whitworth, Milivojevic, Riedewald, McArthur.

Albion: Sanchez, Veltman, Dunk, Webster (Lamptey 75), Estupinan, March, Gross, Mac Allister, Caicedo, Mitoma, Undav (Ferguson 57). **Unused subs:** Steele, Sarmiento, Enciso, Ayari, van Hecke, Buonanotte, Moran.

Match Preview

Our 99th league meeting against Patrick Vieira's men represented a chance for us to make it five Premier League games unbeaten.

With three wins in our last four, we headed into the game looking to cement our place in sixth spot and cut into Tottenham's five-point lead on us in fifth. We also had two games in hand over Antonio Conte's men.

Having scored in nine of our ten games on the road, we sat joint third in the away record table, bagging half of our 34 points away from the Amex, three of which had come the previous weekend when Kaoru Mitoma nodded in a late winner against Bournemouth.

Palace had lost five of their last eight, securing just one win in that sequence — although five of those games have come against four teams in the top four (Manchester United (twice), Newcastle United, Chelsea and Tottenham).

Regarding our team news, De Zerbi confirmed that whilst Colwill and Lallana weren't available, Alexis Mac Allister was, after the Argentinian served a one-match ban for picking up five yellow cards.

It was strange to be playing Palace for the first time this season in mid-February.

And it was the usual attrition.

AMERICAN EXPRESS
cinch

cinch
AMERICAN EXPRESS
HUGHES
25

Pre-Match Ryhme

A blue & white army is heading north.
Oh, our away support.
Our games against Palace mean so much,
And often become a little fraught.

They'll remind Selhurst Park that Sussex by the sea,
Is where you can find us on the map.
And ask the home fans, "Why did you let it bounce?",
And remind them about the 10-point gap.

In-Match Rhymes

1m: KICK-OFF

To improve further,
Our league position.
Claiming points at Palace,
Is our mission.

↓

11m: BIG CHANCE FOR MAC ALLISTER

First proper chance,
Of the game.
But Alexis' side-foot shot.
Is rather tame.

↓

18m: MAC ALLISTER DENIED AGAIN!

Gross to Undav,
Alexis in space.
He could already,
Have claimed a brace!

↓

26m: GUAITA SAVES PALACE AGAIN

March to Mitoma,
Lovely play.
Kaoru's curling right-foot effort,
Is palmed away.

↓

28m: WEBSTER NODS WIDE

Superb Solly,
What a ball!
Adam stretching,
A close call.

32m: ESTUPINAN GOAL RULED OUT BY VAR

A good goal is ruled out,
VAR the offender.
I'm sure they didn't measure offside,
From the last defender!!!

↓

43m: VITAL BLOCK FROM WEBSTER

Palace chance,
But the result's the same.
Adam's second last-ditch tackle,
Of the game.

↓

HALF-TIME RHYME

Plenty of chances,
So far today.
Let's hope in the second half,
We make them pay.

↓

51m: WE'RE PRESSING

Undav to March,
Pressure applied.
Pervis' shot,
Deflected wide.

↓

63m: SOOOOOOOOOLLLLLYYYYYYY! (0-1)

Deadlock broken!
It's bundled in.
At the back post,
Now let's go on and win!

64m: SHHHHHHH!

Home crowd quiet,
Solly quips.
Places his finger,
To his lips.

↓

69m: PALACE LEVEL (1-1)

A worse error by Sanchez,
I cannot recall.
His head is in his hands,
Instead of the ball.

↓

75m: ALEXIS WITH A 25-YARD FREE KICK

Solly is fouled,
Worth a go, I suppose.
Mac Allister hits it,
But over it goes.

↓

84m: GLORIOUS CHANCE FOR MAC ALLISTER!!

It's a free header,
And he wasn't denied.
No, somehow Alexis,
Heads it just wide!

↓

90+4m: FINAL WHISTLE

The VAR may wonder,
Why fans often deride.
Well, let me tell you, I'm certain,
Pervis wasn't offside.

Post-Match Ryhme

I think tonight it's fair to say,
That Sanchez cost us points.
But then again, most of the time,
He rarely disappoints.

I'm more annoyed with the VAR,
As they screwed up yet again.
But they hide behind a wall of silence,
So, to whom do we complain?

MATCH #27

Saturday, 18 February 2023

Brighton & Hove Albion 0 – 1 Fulham

Competition: **Premier League**
Kick-off: **15.00**
Venue: **The Amex Stadium, Brighton**
Weather: **11, cloudy**
Referee: **Darren England**
Attendance: **31,619**

Squads

Albion: Sanchez, Veltman, Webster (Bounanotte 72), Dunk, Estupinan (Lamptey 62), Caicedo, Mac Allister, March, Gross, Mitoma, Ferguson (Undav 72). **Unused subs:** Steele, Sarmiento, Enciso, Undav, Ayari, van Hecke, Hinshelwood.

Fulham: Leno, Tete, Diop, Ream, Robinsion, Palhinha, Reed, Andreas Pereira (Solomon 82'), Wilson (Carlos Vinícius 62'), Willian, De Cordova-Reid. **Unused subs:** Tosin, Rodák, James, Lukić, Cédric Soares, Duffy, Kurzawa.

Match Preview

It was sixth v seventh as we took on Marco Silva's men at the Amex.

Albion were aiming for three successive home wins in the league for the first time since November 2019. We were unbeaten in our last nine home games against promoted sides, but in five previous Premier League meetings against Fulham, we had yet to win (D3, L2). Fulham had won 2-1 when the sides met in August, with Alexis Mac Allister getting Albion's goal at Craven Cottage.

Fulham had beaten Nottingham Forest 2-0 the previous Saturday, their tenth win of the season - only four clubs in the league had won more matches. They had also won four games on the road, the seventh-best away record in the league.

With 11 league goals in 19 games, Serbia striker Aleksandar Mitrovic has played a big part in helping Fulham to sustain their challenge for Europe. The 28-year-old, who scored twice at the World Cup late last year, has netted 35 top-flight goals and contributed 11 assists. His league goals this season include five away from home.

The team news was that Adam Lallana, Danny Welbeck, Billy Gilmour and Levi Colwill were all sidelined, but Roberto De Zerbi confirmed everyone else was available.

Fulham, eh?

AMERICAN EXPRESS
13
34
28

AMERICAN EXPRESS
W88

AMERICAN EXPRESS
CAICEDO
25
6

MARCH
7
VELTMAN
34
TETE
2
J.PALHINHA
26
13
AMERICAN EXPRESS
W88
21
2

Pre-Match Ryhme

A huge game at the Amex,
But, of course, they're all the same.
Three points tomorrow afternoon,
Will, of course, be our aim.

I'll be watching from 4500 miles away,
Hoping that Evan will star.
But one thing I can't accept this week,
Is more dodgy line drawing from VAR.

In-Match Rhymes

1m: KICK-OFF

Middle of February,
Cool and grey.
As Fulham get us,
Underway.

↓

3m: MARCH CURLS ONE JUST WIDE

A great chance,
After a world-class pass,
From Mitoma,
Different class.

↓

17m: DOMINATING?

Yes, OK,
We've yet to score.
But we've 76% possession,
To their 24.

↓

28m: VELTMAN VOLLEY BLOCKED

Pervis pulls one back,
Ends up with Joel.
That would have been,
A lovely goal.

↓

31m: EVAN IS THROUGH!

To beat the keeper to the ball,
Oh, he tries.
Pass a bit too firm,
Leno denies.

HALF-TIME RHYME

Plenty of possession,
But it does not amount,
To any goals,
We have to make it count.

↓

50m: GLORIOUS CHANCE FOR DUNK

Our Captain goes close,
Arguably should have scored.
We're creating loads of chances,
But getting no reward.

↓

54m: PENALTY SHOUT

"Come on ref!",
The north stand beg.
I think Joels sticks out,
A trailing leg.

↓

57m: MARCH'S GOAL RULED OUT

Linesman's decision,
Wasn't hard,
Solly was off,
By at least a yard.

↓

77m: BUONANOTTE GOAL DISALLOWED

Undav the provider,
Unselfish there.
But he's just offside,
Breadth of a hair.

80m: UNDAV HEADS STRAIGHT AT THEIR KEEPER

Oh, my word,
Things are getting taut.
Deniz had more time,
Than he thought.

↓

82m: FULHAM HEAD-INJURY?

They keep going down,
It's pathetic.
I, for one,
Ain't sympathetic.

↓

88m: OH, NO! DISASTER!!! (0-1)

We lost possession,
In the final third.
They score on the break,
Oh, my word.

↓

90+7m: ALEXIS A WHISKER AWAY

We have a free kick,
Seven minutes added on.
It flies just wide,
Our last chance is gone.

↓

90+7m: FINAL WHISTLE

It's what can happen,
In circumstances,
When you dominate,
But don't take your chances.

Post-Match Ryhme

Fulham players get a scuff on the knee,
But they choose to hold their head.
It is complete and utter nonsense,
No wonder it winds up RDZ.

It's like going to the theatre,
But the pitch it is the stage.
And the players have become the actors,
Man, it makes me rage.

MATCH #28

Tuesday, 28 February 2023

Stoke City 0 – 1 Brighton & Hove Albion

Competition: **The FA Cup – fifth round**
Kick-off: **19.15**
Venue: **Bet365 Stadium, Stoke.**
Weather: **6c, cloudy**
Referee: **Darren Bond**
Attendance: **12,949**

Squads

Stoke: Bonham, Sterling (Clucas 68'), Tuanzebe (Taylor 76'), Hoever, Wilmot, Laurent (Smallbone 45'), Thompson, Baker, Brown (Lowe 83'), Tymon, Campbell (Celina 76'). **Unused subs:** Reddin, Clucas, Lowe, Smallbone, Celina, Taylor, Gayle, Fox, Fielding.

Albion: Steele, Gross, Dunk, van Hecke, Lamptey, Sarmiento (Welbeck 78), Caicedo, Buonanotte (Veltman 68), Mac Allister, Mitoma (Encizo 75), Ferguson (Undav 68). **Unused subs:** Sanchez, McGill, Webster, Moran, Hinshelwood.

Match Preview

With wins over Middlesbrough and Liverpool behind us, it was time to see if we could make the sixth round by winning a tricky away tie at the Bet365 Stadium.

We'd faced Stoke City in the fifth round of the FA Cup in 2011, losing 3-0 as the then Premier League Potters went on to reach the final, while we would secure the League One title. Since then, we'd faced each other twice in the top tier, drawing both games in the 2017/18 season — the year Stoke's 10-season stay in the Premier League ended.

Stoke had reached the fifth round of the FA Cup the previous season before losing 2-1 at Crystal Palace. This year they had scored six goals in their two previous FA Cup matches, beating Hartlepool and Stevenage. They sat 17th in the Championship with five wins, four defeats and a draw in their last ten in all competitions. The previous Saturday, Alex Neil's men had gone down 1-0 at home to Millwall, having won three of their previous four games at home.

Roberto De Zerbi had confirmed that we would be without a number of players for the trip to Staffordshire, but that we'd have Danny Welbeck available. He also had confirmed that Lewis Dunk would make his 400th Albion appearance.

Oh, the magic of the cup — and where better to experience it than on a cool Tuesday night in Stoke?

AMERICAN EXPRESS

bet365
AMERICAN EXPRESS
bet365
bet365.com
bet365
AMERICAN EXPRESS

Pre-Match Ryhme

I was very proud this morning,
As at 5am I jumped out of bed,
"Before the game, I need to get some work done",
I told myself in my head.

So I went to the gym, then sat my desk,
Which is often my normal routine,
But in a few minutes, I'll be switching off,
As kick-off here is 13.15.

In-Match Rhymes

0m: APPLAUSE IN MEMORY OF JOHN MOTSON

He painted pictures with words,
Mainly football related.
A seat at the pinnacle of broadcasting,
Has been vacated.

↓

1m: KICK-OFF

Dunk with 400 appearances,
A true Brighton god.
Same as the number of players
In the Chelsea squad.

↓

4m: FABULOUS TACKLE FROM MOISES

Not long ago,
He said he wanted to leave.
Just badly advised,
Is what I believe.

↓

5m: STEELE SAVES FROM CAMPBELL

Stoke not looking,
Intimidated.
Two early chances,
They've created.

↓

7m: STOKE KEEPER SAVES

Great from Tariq,
Back post cross.
Buonanotte with a diving header,
But Bonham's the boss.

29m: STEEL KEEPS OUT A LONG-RANGE EFFORT

In midfield,
The ball Stoke steal.
But luckily, our keeper,
Is the real deal.

↓

31m: EVAN SCORES!!!! (0-1)

Super football,
Tippy tappy.
Evan slots it home,
Better than Mbabbe.

↓

44m: GOOD SAVE FROM STEELE

Thomson's effort,
Was likely going wide.
But keepers have,
No time to decide.

↓

HALF-TIME RHYME

On a wet Tuesday night,
Can you play well in Stoke?
Funny how the saying,
Has become a bit of a joke.

↓

58m: CLOSE FROM SARMIENTO!

Reverse ball from Caicedo,
Jeremy's left-foot strike.
Oh, my dear Moises,
What are you like?

65m: JUST WIDE FROM TUANZEBE

At the back post,
Like a salmon, he rose.
How it didn't go in,
God only knows.

↓

74m: BONHAM SAVES FROM MITOMA

No wonder the ref,
Is getting some stick.
Should be a corner,
But he gives a goal kick.

↓

90+1m: BIG CHANCE FOR UNDAV

Keeper charges out,
But doesn't clear.
Deniz tries a chip from 40 yards,
Oh, so near.

↓

90+2m: CLOSE FROM WELBECK

Undav is unselfish,
Let's the ball run to dat guy,
In space, great connection,
But off the post he sees it fly.

↓

90m+3m: FINAL WHISTLE

Maybe I shouldn't,
But I'm going to say.
We're only one game,
Away from Wem-Ber-Lay!

Post-Match Ryhme

We won in Stoke on a Tuesday night,
On a damp cold night 'n all.
Onwards now to the sixth round,
For those of us who stand or fall.

Congratulations to our captain,
400 appearances, what a man.
Now we turn our focus to the league,
As next up are West Ham.

MATCH #29

Saturday, 4 March 2023

Brighton & Hove Albion 4 – 0 West Ham United

Competition: **Premier League**
Kick-off: **15.00**
Venue: **The Amex Stadium, Brighton**
Weather: **7c, partly sunny**
Referee: **Stuart Attwell**
Attendance: **31,523**

Squads

Albion: Steele, Lamptey (Veltman 15), Webster, Dunk, Estupinan (Welbeck 76), March (Buonanotte 75), Gross, Caicedo, Mitoma (Enciso 84), Mac Allister, Ferguson (Sarmiento 84). **Unused subs:** Sanchez, Undav, Gilmour, van Hecke.

West Ham: Areola, Johnson, Aguerd, Ogbonna (Zouma 68), Emerson, Rice, Souček (Downes 76), Paquetá (Lanzini 76), Bowen, Ings, Benrahma (Fornals 46). **Unused subs:** Anang (GK), Hegyi (GK), Cresswell, Scamacca.

Match Preview

Having only picked up one point from a possible six since beating Bournemouth a month ago, we were looking forward to returning to winning ways at the Amex.

We sat in eighth place and, whilst a victory wouldn't see us improve our league position, it would move us closer to Fulham, who were four points above us, having played three games more.

David Moyes's team sat just two points clear of the bottom three, but a victory could propel them as high as 13th. Interestingly, in the Premier League, West Ham had yet to defeat us — with us winning five of the 11 games played and six ending all square. Away from the Premier League, they were still looking to progress in the Europa Conference League.

Regarding team news, De Zerbi had confirmed that Pervis Estupinan and Solly March would be available to play, as well as Danny Welbeck.

Away from the pitch, Moises Caicedo had just signed an extension to his contract, having previously indicated he would like to leave in the winter transfer window.

And finally, Roberto De Zerbi would not be in the technical area for the game, having received a one-match touchline ban for Breach of FA Rule E3.1 after the 1-0 defeat to Fulham the previous month.

Who wants to be beaten by a beach?

energizer
MITOMA
22

MITOMA
22
AMERICAN EXPRESS
GROSS
13
27
thailandelite

Pre-Match Ryhme

At least tomorrow will be dry,
If you are going to the game.
Although thick clouds will cover the sun,
Which is a real shame.

Moises more than likely starts,
It seems relationships are mended.
Let's hope we can score a goal,
For every year his contract was extended.

In-Match Rhymes

1m: KICK-OFF

Pretty big shock,
When the team sheet came out.
Jason Steele in goal,
Is Roberto's shout.

↓

11m: LOVELY ATTEMPT FROM MARCH

Solly bursts through,
West Ham defenders part.
Super player,
Decent start.

↓

17m: PENALTY TO US!

Bowen clumsy,
Mitoma hits the ground.
West Ham players,
The ref surround.

↓

18m: NO MISTAKE FROM ALEXIS!!! (1-0)

Oh, so clinical,
From the spot,
Any doubt he'd score?
Not a jot!!

↓

24m: STEELE SAVES FROM BOWEN

Only Jason's second,
Premier League start.
But already,
He's playing his part.

31m: FANTASTIC FROM WEBSTER

Smothered a chance,
They created.
Adam Webster,
Underrated,

↓

39m: JOHNSON CLEARS MARCH'S CROSS

Solly fires one in,
Curl and speed.
Mitoma almost,
Extends our lead.

↓

HALF-TIME RHYME

Steele with three,
Important interventions.
An early second-half goal,
Will signal our intentions.

↓

51m: VEELLLTTTMMMAAANNN!!!! (2-0)

We've scored for a corner,
I'm impressed.
And even stranger,
Joel used his chest.

↓

53m: AREOLA SAVES FROM FERGUSON

We're on top,
As things stand.
A bullet from Evan,
Stings their keeper's hand.

69m: MIITTTOOOMMMAAA!!! (3-0)

As a fantastic team goal,
It's high up the list.
Mitoma at the back post!!!!
Gross assist.

↓

80m: MAN OF THE MATCH?

So many players,
Could be nominated.
West Ham being totally,
Dominated.

↓

89m: DANNY MAKES IT FOUR!!!!!!! (4-0)

Welbeck gets his goal,
The Amex rocks.
Bottom left corner,
From the edge of the box.

↓

90+3m: CLOSE FROM GROSS

Pascal Gross,
Did contrive,
With a long-range shot,
To make it five.

↓

90+4m: FINAL WHISTLE

I don't wish to preach,
Or do a big speech.
But for the second time this season,
West Ham have been beaten by a beach.

Post-Match Ryhme

You may be in the pub,
You may be heading to bed.
You may be out with loads of friends,
Or home alone instead.

It doesn't really matter,
As long as tonight, you please remember.
That you're part of a family of worldwide fans,
Whose team are on course to play in Europe come September.

MATCH #30

Saturday, 11 March 2023

Leeds United 2 – 2 Brighton & Hove Albion

Competition: **Premier League**
Kick-off: **15.00**
Venue: **Elland Road, Leeds**
Weather: **4c, cloudy**
Referee: **Paul Tierney**
Attendance: **36, 471**

Squads

Leeds: Meslier, Ayling, Firpo, Koch, Aaronson (Rutter 84'), Roca (McKennie 66'), Bamford (Rodrigo 66'), Summerville (Gnonto 66'), Harrison (Sinisterra 90'), Adams, Wober. **Unused subs:** Robles, Struijk, Kristensen, Greenwood.

Albion: Steele, Veltman, Dunk, Webster (van Hecke 85), Estupinan, Gross, March, Caicedo, Mitoma, Mac Allister, Ferguson (Welbeck 67). **Unused subs:** Sanchez, Colwill, Sarmiento, Enciso, Undav, Ayari, Bounanotte.

Match Preview

Albion were looking to make it six games unbeaten as our fantastic away support headed up to Elland Rd on this cold Saturday afternoon.

Since their promotion to the Premier League, the Whites had only taken two points off us, losing the other three encounters — including our 1-0 win against them in August 2022 at the Amex.

Jesse Marsch was in charge of Leeds that day but had since been replaced by Javi Gracia, with the Spaniard charged with turning around their fortunes. It was a big task as they sat just outside the relegation zone on goal difference.

Their form at Elland Road had kept the bottom three in the Premier League at arm's length with four wins and four draws in 12 home matches, but one win on the road is form that would have to improve if Leeds were to climb the table.

On the other hand, we sat eight with 38 points and hadn't lost an away Premier League game since the trip to Manchester City at the end of October, winning three and drawing twice on the road since.

As well as suggesting that Jason Steele would retain his place in the starting line-up, Roberto De Zerbi confirmed that Solly March was fit and ready for the game but that he had yet to decide on whether or not to include Levi Colwill or Tariq Lamptey.

This one would be tough.

AMERICAN EXPRESS
SBOTOP
AMERICAN EXPRESS
SBOTOP
AMERICAN EXPRESS
AMERICAN EXPRESS
30

Pre-Match Ryhme

Come on the boys from Brighton,

Yes, I know it's cold.

But we're pushing for Europe and on De Zerbi's line-up

I am really sold.

I see Liverpool have just gone behind,

And if Bournemouth can survive,

It would mean we'd be just a point behind them,

Before the clock strikes five.

In-Match Rhymes

1m: KICK-OFF

Elland Rd,

Man, it's bouncing.

Can we give,

Leeds a trouncing?

↓

5m: HOME CROWD AGITATED

We have the ball,

At the back.

Leeds not pressing,

They just don't attack.

↓

15m: VELTMAN EFFORT DEFLECTED WIDE

Not too many chances,

Early doors.

But we have a corner,

The away support roars.

↓

18m: ALBION CARVE LEEDS OPEN

Like a Turkey at Christmas,

It is great to see.

I predict the Leeds defence,

Will let in three.

↓

33m: GOAL!! MAC ALLISTER!! (0-1)

Lovely play,

Cross from Gross.

Mitoma nods it back,

Alexis near post.

40m: BANFORD EQUALISES (1-1)

They haven't looked,

A real threat.

Underside of the crossbar,

Roof of the net.

↓

43m: HUGE CHANCE FOR MAC ALLISTER

Great from Mitoma,

Pressure applied.

First time from Alexis,

But puts it wide.

↓

HALF-TIME RHYME

Superb half,

Mainly in control.

Just one small mistake,

Led to their goal.

↓

48m: VITAL TOUCH FROM STEELE

Leeds' Aaronson,

First, he trips.

But then shoots goalward,

Fingertips.

↓

58m: GREAT OPPORTUNITY FOR AYLING

Head in his hands,

On the floor.

Half-volley flies over,

Should really score.

61m: WE'RE AHEAD!!! (1-2)

Is that Solly's?

Or an OG?

I actually don't care,

Now let's get three!!

↓

74m: TWO SAVES FROM MESLIER

Leeds' young keeper,

Doing well.

Alexis and Solly,

He does repel.

↓

78m: LEEDS BACK LEVEL (2-2)

Leeds play a short corner,

Harrison swings a boot.

Flies over Steele,

Our support now mute.

↓

85m: A BREAK COMES TO NOTHING

Mitoma sprinting,

The lad has pace.

Needed an early ball,

To reach March in space.

↓

90+5m: FINAL WHISTLE

Entertaining game,

A point away.

Leeds will be going down,

If they play that way.

Post-Match Ryhme

If I'm going to be really candid,

I'm a little frustrated that we drew.

I think our performance deserved all three points,

But that's probably a biased point of view.

On the positive side, I see Liverpool lost,

And I've just learnt that Brentford, they did too.

So if Palace lose, our day will be complete,

And let's be honest, they usually do.

MATCH #31

Wednesday, 15 March 2023

Brighton & Hove Albion 1 – 0 Crystal Palace

Competition: **Premier League**
Kick-off: **15.30**
Venue: **The Amex Stadium, Brighton**
Weather: **8c, drizzle**
Referee: **Peter Bankes**
Attendance: **30,933**

Squads

Albion: Steele, Veltman, Dunk, Colwill, Estupinan, Caicedo, Gross, March (Webster 90), Mac Allister (Sarmiento 88), Mitoma (Enciso 79), Welbeck (Ferguson 79). **Unused subs:** Sanchez, Undav, Gilmour, van Hecke, Buonanotte.

Palace: Whitworth, Clyne, Andersen, Guéhi, Mitchell, Doucouré (Eze 45), Lokonga, Schlupp (Ahamada 80), Olise (Ayew 70), Zaha, Edouard (Mateta 80). **Unused subs:** Goodman, Ward, Tomkins, Richards, Milivojevic.

Match Preview

Albion welcomed the old enemy to the Amex for this Wednesday evening kick-off, just a month after we'd drawn 1-1 with Patrick Vieira's side in south London.

We'd suffered our first defeat of 2023 the following week against Fulham but had continued to impress, putting four past West Ham without reply in our next game at the Amex before taking a deserved point at Leeds United.

We were six points better off after 24 games than in any other top-flight season, and our volume of goals had been an essential factor in that. We currently averaged 1.875 per game (45 in 24 games), and this was likely to prove crucial against a Palace team who hadn't managed a shot on target in their last three league matches.

Without a win this calendar year, Palace had slowly been dragged towards the relegation battle, but their fine form in the first half of the season meant they were in pole position to pull away from danger. They were 12th with a superior goal difference to five of the eight teams below them.

A win for Palace would go a long way towards alleviating relegation fears, whilst a victory for Albion would see us move level on points with sixth-placed Liverpool.

Tariq Lamptey's fitness was to be assessed ahead of the game after being substituted with an injury against West Ham earlier in the month.

I was flying back to Europe the day of the game and ended up watching much of it from Dallas Forth Worth airport.

AMERICAN EXPRESS
AMERICAN EXPRESS

Pre-Match Ryhme

I'm on a plane and about to take off,
The first of my two flights heads to Dallas.
But instead, I wish I was back in Brighton,
Having a beer as we prepare for Palace.

At least it's quite a short flight,
So when I land, I'll be sprinting off the plane.
And heading to the airport's biggest sports bar,
Where I can hopefully watch the game.

In-Match Rhymes

1m: KICK-OFF

No shots on target,
For three full games.
I hope that Palace stat,
Remains the same.

↓

1m: ZAHA DENIED

It seems I tempted fate,
Our defence in a spin.
Steele saves,
But that was going in.

↓

7m: EDOUARD GOES CLOSE

We've got away with one,
Without a doubt.
A free header,
Six yards out.

↓

8m: A HAT-TRICK OF PALACE CHANCES

Steele saves again,
A one-on-one.
And less than nine minutes since,
The game begun.

↓

15m: SOOOOOLLLLLLLYYYY!!!! (1-0)

The Palace midfield,
Mitoma burst through.
On a plate for Solly,
NOW LET'S TURN THE SCREW!!

16m: IT'S RAINING CATS AND DOGS

Just before,
The deadlock was broken.
It started to spit,
Then the heavens opened.

↓

19m: DOUCOURE DENIES DANNY

Pascal cuts one back,
Welbeck's there.
Plenty of chances,
Feisty affair.

↓

35m: EDOUARD THROUGH AGAIN

The rain helped us out,
One has to feel.
As the through ball skidded,
Straight through to Steele.

↓

HALF-TIME RHYME

Well done, Palace,
Applause from our crowd.
You managed some shots on target,
You must be very proud.

↓

51m: PERVIS DENIED BY WHITWORTH

Alexis bursts through,
Pervis in his way.
Keeper saves with his foot,
I wish we'd made them pay.

53m: POWER CUT CAUSES BRIEF STOPPAGE

We had no floodlights,
Was the news.
But it seems the Amex's sparky,
Brought along a spare fuse.

↓

66m: BRILLIANT SAVE FROM WHITWORTH

An out-swinging corner,
Alexis connects.
His downward header is powerful,
But the keeper's right hand deflects.

↓

85m: CLOSE FROM ALEXIS

Through the Palace defence,
Mac Allister bobs and weaves.
His shot flies just wide,
Huge applause received.

↓

90+5: CAREFUL, LADS!!!'

Near calamity at the back,
Things almost went south.
Prompting an expletive,
To come out of my mouth.

↓

90+10m: FINAL WHISTLE

Those added minutes,
Were a real drag.
But all that matters?
THREE POINTS IN THE BAG!!!

Post-Match Ryhme

I had to turn my phone off,
And missed the last few minutes of the game.
As a call came from the flight crew,
While we were taxiing on the plane.

"We're next in line for take-off,
Please put your phones in in-flight mode."
But as soon as I got the on-board Wi-Fi,
I saw the result, and champagne flowed!!

MATCH #32

Sunday, 19 March 2023

Brighton & Hove Albion 5 – 0 Grimsby Town

Competition: **The FA Cup – quarter-final**
Kick-off: **14.15**
Venue: **The Amex Stadium, Brighton**
Weather: **10c, partly sunny**
Referee: **Jarred Gillett**
Attendance: **29,415**

Squads

Albion: Sanchez, Gross, Webster, Dunk (van Hecke 77), Estupinan (Colwill 45), Caicedo, Mac Allister (Ayari 77), March, Mitoma, Undav (Sarmiento 72), Ferguson (Welbeck 72). **Unused subs:** Steele, Enciso, Veltman, Buonanotte.

Grimsby: Crocombe, Efete, Smith, Waterfall, Maher, Driscoll-Glennon, Clifton (Morris 71), Green (Hunt 45), Holohan (Khouri 84), Khan (Taylor 71), Orsi-Dadomo (McAtee 45). **Unused subs:** Pearson, Emmanuel, Battersby, Amos.

Match Preview

Albion were looking to secure a place in the semi-final of the Emirates FA Cup with victory in this early afternoon tie.

We'd beaten Middlesbrough 5-1, Liverpool 2-1, and Stoke City 1-0 to reach this stage of the competition, putting us within touching distance of the last four, which we had last achieved in 2019.

Having started in the first round, the Mariners' run to this stage had been impressive. Plymouth, Cambridge and Burton (all from League One) had been beaten before Championship side Luton Town were defeated 3-0 in a fourth round replay. This was followed by a famous 2-1 victory over Premier League Southampton at St Mary's.

Paul Hurst's team had also been in decent league form, suffering only one defeat in their last seven League Two matches and winning their last two.

We were looking to continue a run of form that has seen us lose only once in 12 matches in all competitions in 2023. Since a 1-0 home defeat to Fulham, we'd beaten West Ham and Crystal Palace, with a draw with Leeds United sandwiched in between.

Although we'd last come up against them in the league in 2002, the game represented the first time we had faced Grimsby in the FA Cup since January 1930 — a third round tie which the Albion won after a replay — at a time when we were in the Third Division South while the Mariners were a top-flight side.

We entered the match with Tariq Lamptey ruled out, along with longer-term absentees Adam Lallana and Jakub Moder.

TOOLS

MITOMA
22
myenergi

AMERICAN EXPRESS
UNIBET

AMERICAN EXPRESS
28
22
21
13
10

Pre-Match Ryhme

Who else is ready to play Grimsby,
Tomorrow afternoon,
And take a step nearer an FA Cup final,
On the 3rd of June?

Imagine getting to the final,
I'm sure many would shed a tear.
Finally, a chance to avenge 'that' loss,
From four decades ago this year.

In-Match Rhymes

1m: KICK-OFF

As we kick-off,
One thing is clear.
Cup magic is alive,
What an atmosphere!

↓

6m: UNDAV PUTS US AHEAD! (1-0)

Moises' long-range shot,
Bounces along the ground.
Their keeper saves,
Deniz on the rebound.

↓

20m: HARD TO BREAK DOWN

Grimsby sitting deep,
And getting deeper.
But we've had no more chances,
To test their keeper.

↓

32m: OUTSIDE HIS BOX?

Sanchez gathers,
Over the line?
VAR decides,
That it was fine.

↓

33m: A MISS FROM MITOMA!

As Kaoru stretches,
An unusual sight.
Should have used his left,
Tried to use his right.

HALF-TIME RHYME

We've created chances,
Pretty well we've done,
But find ourselves.
Only ahead by one.

↓

48m: IT IS ALMOST TWO!!

Solly's deflected cross,
Loops over the keeper's head.
Hits the post, then Deniz,
Puts it in row Z.

↓

51m: FERGUSON MAKES IT 2-0!!!!!! (2-0)

Bottom corner,
Can we agree,
Some of the best close control,
One will ever see?

↓

55m: CLOSE FROM MITOMA

Probably the fastest player,
From either side.
Side-foots an effort,
Rolls just wide.

↓

67m: WEBSTER HITS THE CROSSBAR

Corner comes in,
Adam stars.
Pretty useful in their box,
As well as ours.

70m: EVAN HAS HIS BRACE! (3-0)

Lovely footwork from Undav,
Just sublime.
No offside flag,
Not this time.

↓

82m: MARCH HEADS IN!!! (4-0)

Webster crosses,
Solly arriving.
Not easy to do,
Whilst you're diving.

↓

85m: SUPERB SANCHEZ SAVE

Out of nothing,
Half a chance.
Grimsby can't win,
But they still advance.

↓

90m: MITOMA ADDS ANOTHER!!! (5-0)

Sarmiento picks,
Their defender's pocket.
Ball slowly rolls over the line,
Certainly was not a rocket.

↓

90+2m: FINAL WHISTLE

We scored five,
We missed a few.
But who cares,
As we're going through!!!

Post-Match Ryhme

A message to all you Mariners,
I hope you get back home alright.
Great support and good to share,
A few beers in the pub with you all last night.

Thousands came down from up north,
You did Grimsby proud.
Waving haddocks and singing your songs,
Blimey, you were loud!

MATCH #33

Saturday, 1 April 2023

Brighton & Hove Albion 3 – 3 Brentford

Competition: **Premier League**
Kick-off: **15.00**
Venue: **The Amex Stadium, Brighton**
Weather: **13c, partly sunny**
Referee: **Michael Oliver**
Attendance: **31,493**

Squads

Albion: Steele, Veltman (Enciso 72), Dunk, Colwill, Estupinan (Buonanotte 83), Gross, Caicedo, March, Mac Allister, Mitoma, Welbeck (Undav 83). **Unused subs:** Sanchez, Webster, Ayari, Gilmour, van Hecke, Moran.

Brentford: Raya; Hickey, Jansson, Pinnock, Mee, Henry; Norgaard, Jensen (Ghoddos 85), Damsgaard (Dasilva 73); Mbeumo (Wissa 79), Toney. **Unused subs:** Strakosha, Schade, Zanka, Roerslev, Stevens, Olakigbe.

Match Preview

With only one defeat in the league this year, we were looking to make it three consecutive wins in all competitions, having beaten Crystal Palace and Grimsby Town before the international break.

With Liverpool having been beaten 4 -1 at Manchester City in the 12.30 kick-off earlier in the day, we entered the game knowing that victory would move up to sixth in the Premier League — four points off fourth place Tottenham, with two games in hand.

Brentford were one of the six teams that had beaten us in the league this season and were on level on points with us (42), although they had played two more games.

A similar run of form had seen them lose just once in 2023, while wins this season against Manchester City and Liverpool, as well as a draw with league leaders Arsenal, reflected the fine season Thomas Frank's team were enjoying.

Contrasting styles were likely to be on show at the Amex, though. Albion had enjoyed the second-highest possession in the Premier League thus far this season with 60.8%, while Brentford had the fourth lowest, 43%.

Our team news was dominated by the announcement that Jeremy Sarmiento would be missing for an extended period, having picked up an injury while on international duty with Ecuador.

AMERICAN EXPRESS
HOLLYWOOD
JENSEN

Pre-Match Ryhme

It's fantastic that Wembley beckons,
But it's important not to lose sight.
That when it comes to Europe,
Things still are still really tight.

All eyes turn to this afternoon,
Remember, Brentford aren't that bad.
And we need to pick up points in games like this,
If we want to play the likes of Real Sociedad.

In-Match Rhymes

1m: KICK-OFF

As the sun dries out,
The damp and wet.
We want a different winner,
To the one last time we met.

↓

5m: GREAT CHANCE FOR ALBION!

Mitoma's through!
With speed advances.
Defender blocks,
But some early chances.

↓

10m: GOAL TO BRENTFORD (0-1)

A powerful header,
Their first attack.
Caught us cold,
At the back.

↓

12m: CHEWING GUM

The fastest chewer.
I ever saw.
Thomas Frank,
Doesn't it hurt his jaw?

↓

21m: ROUTE ONE, BUT WE'RE LEVEL! (1-1)

His satisfaction,
He can't conceal!
A lob from Mitoma,
An assist from Steele!

22m: BRENTFORD BACK IN FRONT (1-2)

Toney from close range,
Brentford's lead restored.
"You're at your most vulnerable,
When you've just scored."

↓

28m: WELBZ LEVELS IT!! (2-2)

Albion are putting us,
Through the shredder.
Solly's deep cross,
DANNY'S DOWNWARD HEADER!

↓

33m: CHANCES AT BOTH ENDS

Pontus Jansson close,
With a bicycle kick.
Then Solly's crosses,
Kaoru can't get a nick.

↓

44m: GREAT SAVE

Alexis Mac Allister,
What a player.
Fierce right-foot shot,
Pushed away by Raya.

↓

HALF-TIME RHYME

Decent game,
Both sides a threat.
I'm forecasting,
More goals in this yet.

49m: BRENTFORD AHEAD (2-3)

Such a simple goal,
That wasn't in our plan.
Deep free kick,
I think Pervis lost his man.

↓

67m: MULTIPLE SAVES BY RAYA

From Pascal, Solly,
Caicedo too.
My fingernails,
I've begun to chew.

↓

71m: DUNK SO CLOSE WITH A HEADER!!

The north stand rose,
In anticipation!
Lewis kicks the post,
In frustration.

↓

90m: VAR! PENALTY! ALL SQUARE! (3-3)

Hickey handballs,
Alexis to take.
High to the right,
MAKES NO MISTAKE!!

↓

90+7m: FINAL WHISTLE

A point gained,
It seems to me.
Just don't look too closely,
At XG.

Post-Match Ryhme

I must admit to hating playing Brentford,
So glad they are out of sight.
And that we can now focus on the game,
Against Bournemouth on Tuesday night.

The good news is that Fulham lost,
And Liverpool got thrashed by City too.
We're up to sixth, on the league transfixed,
As Europe, we pursue.

MATCH #34

Tuesday, 4 April 2023

AFC Bournemouth 0 – 2 Brighton & Hove Albion

Competition: **Premier League**
Kick-off: **19.45**
Venue: **The Vitality Stadium, Bournemouth**
Weather: **8c, clear**
Referee: **Darren Bond**
Attendance: **10,266**

Squads

Bournemouth: Neto, Smith, Stephens, Senesi (Zabarnyi, 84), Kelly, Lerma, Billing (Semenyo, 84), Ouattara (Cook, 84), Traorè (Brooks, 72), Christie (Tavernier, 58), Solanke. **Unused subs:** Travers, Anthony, Viña, Rothwell.

Albion: Steele, Veltman, Dunk, Webster, Estupinan, Mac Allister (Enciso 73), Gross, March, Caicedo (Ayari 80), Mitoma (Undav 90+2), Ferguson (Welbeck 73). **Unused subs:** Sanchez, Colwill, Gilmour, van Hecke, Buonanotte.

Match Preview

With the run-in to the end of the season very much upon us, we headed to the Vitality Stadium looking to make it five consecutive Premier League games unbeaten going into this Tuesday night game.

Whilst, arguably, some would have felt somewhat frustrated with a point, our 3-3 draw with Brentford three days earlier had continued our fine run of form in 2023. We had only suffered one Premier League defeat this year.

Equally impressive was our form on the road. Our visit to Manchester City in October was the last time Albion had been beaten away from home, with three wins and four draws since.

Whilst a win wouldn't see us move in the table, it would help us increase the points gap from the chasing pack of Brentford, Liverpool and Aston Villa in the search of European football.

On the other hand, three points for Bournemouth would move them up to 13th, their highest position since match week 12. It would also pull them four points clear of the bottom three in what continued to be one of the most intense relegation battles the Premier League had seen.

Runs of defeats for Gary O'Neil's men had hampered their first season back in the top-flight, but two wins in their last three games against Liverpool and Fulham had breathed new life into their hopes of survival.

Unfortunately, ongoing issues with Tariq Lamptey's fitness meant he wouldn't be available for us, but Roberto De Zerbi had confirmed Evan Ferguson would be fit and available, having missed out on the squad last time out.

CHRISTIE
10

WEBSTER
MITOMA
SPCAPITAL
STADIUM
VITALITY

VELTMAN
ESTUPIÑAN
AYARI
VITALITY STADIUM
0-2

Pre-Match Ryhme

I've just shut down my computer,
And turned my TV on.
I am encouraged by our line-up,
Man, it looks really strong.

It is great to think that around the world,
Thousands of seagulls are tuning in.
To watch this game being played along the coast,
And one we really need to win.

In-Match Rhymes

1m: KICK-OFF

I'm pretty busy workwise,
So was at my desk by four.
But now that we are underway,
I'm not working anymore.

↓

3m: MAC ALLISTER HAMMERS OVER

At least two tackles,
Did Alexis ride.
But his powerful shot,
Goes high and wide.

↓

14m: CHANCE FOR THE HOSTS

What just happened?
A corner taken quick.
Stephens tried to head with power,
But just got a flick.

↓

23m: GLENN MURRAY ON TV

Whilst we push forward,
With attacking intent.
Muzza suggests our missed chances,
We may lament.

↓

28m: INCREDIBLE FINISH FROM EVAN!! (0-1)

Call it a flick,
Or a back heel.
WHAT IN THE WORLD!!?
Oh man, how must he feel?

36m: SOLID SAVE FROM STEELE

Mistake from Moises,
Who loses possession.
But Steele ensures nothing,
Comes from his transgression.

↓

38m: BIG MISS FROM OUATTARA

How did he miss?
I just don't know.
He chose to flick it,
With his toe.

↓

39m: STEELE SAVES, WEBSTER BLOCKS

It's all hands on deck,
At the back.
As we successfully defuse,
Bournemouth's attack.

↓

HALF-TIME RHYME

Early on,
It was hard work.
But what a finish by Evan!
I went berserk.

↓

46m: FERGUSON BENDS IT JUST WIDE

He's a special talent,
Bournemouth can't subdue.
Evan almost,
Puts us up by two.

50m: STEELE TIPS ONE OVER THE BAR

Lerma's effort,
Hit with thunder.
And I think.
It was dipping under.

↓

55m: FERGUSON FIRES OVER

A lovely move,
No reward.
But so much easier,
Than the one he scored!

↓

76m, 83M & 88M: GOOD SAVES FROM NETO

We're creating chances,
Bournemouth dropping deeper,
Just can't seem,
To beat their keeper.

↓

90+1m: ENCISO!!!!!!!!!!!!!!!!!! (0-2)

His first PL goal!!
Ensures the win.
So level-headed,
Calmly rolled it in!!

↓

90+7m: FINAL WHISTLE

Bournemouth played well,
But just couldn't score.
I wouldn't have argued,
If it had finished a draw.

Post-Match Ryhme

What a fantastic duo,
Evan & Julio are.
So many years ahead of them,
When hopefully, for us, they'll star.

But I have just worked something out,
Yes, if my maths is correct, it appears,
That the combined age of them both,
Is still less than me by 14 years!!!

MATCH #35

Saturday, 8 April 2023

Tottenham Hotspur 2 – 1 Brighton & Hove Albion

Competition: **Premier League**
Kick-off: **15.00**
Venue: **The Tottenham Hotspur Stadium, London**
Weather: **15c, mainly sunny**
Referee: **Stuart Attwell**
Attendance: **61,405**

Squads

Spurs: Lloris, Romero, Dier, Lenglet, Pedro Porro, Hojbjerg, Skipp (Sarr 88), Perisic (Tanganga 90+2), Kulusevski (Danjuma 78), Kane, Son. **Unused subs:** Forster, Austin, Sanchez, Devine, Mundle, Richarlison.

Albion: Steele, Veltman (Enciso 85), Dunk, Colwill (Webster 69), Estupinan, Gross, Caicedo, March, Mac Allister, Mitoma, Welbeck (Ferguson 66). **Unused subs:** Sanchez, Undav, Ayari, Gilmour, van Hecke, Buonanotte.

Match Preview

Albion were looking to close the gap on fourth-place Tottenham after we had extended our unbeaten run on the road to seven games the previous Tuesday night with a 2-0 victory at Bournemouth. It was a sequence that started at Wolves in November and was form that had been integral in our attempt to qualify for Europe for the first time.

We were sitting in sixth spot, and a win would see us move to within a point of Tottenham, who had yet to move out of the top five all season. On their part, a Tottenham win would potentially see them move above Newcastle and into third.

The game presented Kaoru Mitoma with the opportunity to build on his record-breaking run for Albion. His assist for Evan Ferguson at Bournemouth marked the fifth consecutive game the Japan international had been directly involved in a goal, the first time an Albion player has managed to do so in the top-flight.

Spurs' previous manager Antonio Conte had departed in March, and his assistant manager Cristian Stellini had taken over in a caretaker role. His first game in charge had been the previous Monday when his team conceded a late equaliser against Everton at Goodison Park after Harry Kane put them ahead with a penalty.

Head coach Roberto De Zerbi had confirmed that midfielders Moises Caicedo and Alexis Mac Allister were both fit to face Tottenham. Tariq Lamptey and Adam Lallana were still absent through injury.

The game marked the chance for Lewis Dunk to become the first Albion player to reach 200 Premier League appearances.

AMERICAN EXPRESS
13
29
CAICEDO
25
23
33:07

JOD
22
GROSS
13
AMERICAN EXPRESS
AMERICAN EXPRESS
6
22
25

Pre-Match Ryhme

No doubt Kane is a fantastic player,
But is he on the wane?
Soon he'll hit the magic 30,
How long at his peak can he remain?

Today we're off to play his team,
And hoping to put on a show.
Whatever we do, we mustn't breathe near Harry,
Or he'll go down, you know.

In-Match Rhymes

1m: KICK-OFF

We can't imagine,
The team without,
Lewis Dunk,
200 not out.

↓

6m: SURELY HANDBALL IN THE AREA?!

Gross with a corner,
Melee in the box.
With Lenglet's hand,
The ball gets knocked.

↓

10m: UNBELIEVABLE GOAL FROM SON (1-0)

Son's form this season
Has not been good.
But against us, he scores a worldly,
You just knew he would.

↓

17m: MITOMA'S GOAL DISALLOWED

VAR decides its handball,
After a lengthy delay.
But not the one earlier,
Decisions not going our way.

↓

26m: CAICEDO HITS THE POST

After Lloris makes a save,
Moises lets one fly.
I think Lloris touched that too,
It's been a good reply.

28m: GREAT TACKLE BY DUNK

Hojbjerg down the left,
Edge of the box.
Lewis steams in,
And his shot blocks.

↓

34m: AND NOW LEWIS SCORES!!!!! (1-1)

A Gross corner,
Terrible marking.
Dunk's powerful header,
Are we on a comeback embarking?

↓

HALF-TIME RHYME

I'm so frustrated,
The ref's eyes deceived.
The Mitoma handball,
Needs to be seen to be believed

↓

55m: WELBECK'S GOAL RULED OUT

What's with our luck?
False alarm.
VAR says Danny's shot,
Hit Mac Allister's arm.

↓

59m: BOTH MANAGERS SENT OFF

Lots of touchline agro.
Why? I've no clue.
And whilst I don't know much Italian,
I'm pretty sure the language turned blue.

64m: KANE BLAZES OVER

Our admin just posted,
'This is stressful'.
Shot from Kane,
Is unsuccessful.

↓

72m: VAR GOES AWOL. RIDICULOUS!!!!

Mitoma's foot gets stood on!!
How come the ref can't perceive it?
It's a bloody stonewall penalty!!!
The TV commentators can't believe it!!!!!!

↓

79m: KANE GIVES SPURS THE LEAD (2-1)

If it wasn't so serious,
It would be quite amusing.
The officials have been atrocious,
We should not be losing.

↓

82m: DUNK NODS OVER

Nearly a carbon copy,
Of his earlier goal.
Can't get Solly's corner,
Under control.

↓

90+7m: FINAL WHISTLE

It's a refereeing farce,
A complete circus.
VAR is simply,
Not fit for purpose.

Post-Match Ryhme

I'm sure every referee does their best,
And, of course, they enjoy their fame.
But one of the problems, in my opinion,
Is that too few have played the game.

I wonder if we'll get an apology,
For today's complete & utter farce?
As of right now from me, my response it would be,
"You can stick it up your ...."

MATCH #36

Saturday, 15 April 2023

Chelsea 1 – 2 Brighton & Hove Albion

Competition: **Premier League**
Kick-off: **15.00**
Venue: **Stamford Bridge, London**
Weather: **15c, scattered clouds**
Referee: **Robert Jones**
Attendance: **40,126**

Squads

Chelsea: Kepa, Chalobah, W. Fofana (James 57), Badiashile, Chilwell, Zakaria (Mount 74), Enzo (Kovacic 57), Pulisic (Ziyech 57), Gallagher, Mudryk, Sterling (Joao Felix 57). **Unused subs:** Mendy, Azpilicueta, Cucurella, Aubameyang.

Albion: Sanchez, Veltman (Enciso 27), Webster (van Hecke 87), Dunk, Estupinan, Gross, March, Caicedo, Mitoma, Mac Allister, Ferguson (Welbeck 39). **Unused subs:** McGill, Undav, Gilmour, Buonanotte, Offiah, Moran.

Match Preview

Albion looked to return to winning ways as we headed to Stamford Bridge.

The match marked a quick return to London for Albion, who were on the end of some outrageous decisions (in my opinion) from the officials last time out when we had lost 2-1 at Tottenham the previous weekend.

That fixture had marked just our second league defeat of 2023, having last been beaten in mid-February by Fulham.

That strong form had maintained our place in seventh spot in the Premier League, but following Aston Villa's somewhat surprising 3-0 defeat of Newcastle at Villa Park in the early game, we knew that even a victory wouldn't impact our position.

We could take heart from the fact we hadn't lost to a team currently in the bottom ten — winning 11 of our 15 games so far, including a 4-1 win over Chelsea in October. Back then, the Blues had been led out by Graham Potter, who had departed the Amex for Stamford Bridge the month before, but Potter had since left Chelsea, and Frank Lampard had taken over in a caretaker role until the end of the season.

The Blues' record goalscorer had overseen two matches so far, losing 1-0 at Wolves in the league and 2-0 at Real Madrid in the Champions League.

Those results had been part of a challenging run for Chelsea, who were winless in their last four Premier League games. A victory would lift them move up a place to tenth.

Regarding team news, Roberto De Zerbi had indicated he'd be making a few last-minute calls on the morning of the game.

CHILWELL
21

AMERICAN EXPRESS

Pre-Match Ryhme

Part of me would slightly prefer it,
If Potter was still manager there.
But I suppose if I'm being logical,
It won't affect how we prepare.

Frank Lampard is the guy in charge,
Many are surprised he's back at the Bridge.
Two-nil, I think, and then I'll get to drink,
The beers I've got cooling in the fridge.

In-Match Rhymes

1m: KICK-OFF

Hoping VAR,
Has a better day.
And we get,
A win away.

↓

3m: MAC ALLISTER JUST WIDE

Chelsea defence,
Already sweating.
Alexis hits,
The side netting.

↓

6m: CLOSE TO AN OG

An outstretched leg
Lewis does extend.
Nearly scores,
At the wrong end!

↓

9m: FERGUSON HITS THE CROSSBAR

What a hectic start,
We have today.
Evan, right-footed,
Booted away.

↓

13m: CHELSEA TAKE THE LEAD (1-0)

Gallagher's shot,
Did deflect,
Sanchez wrong-footed,
Could not correct.

25m: MARCH SMASHES ONE JUST OVER

Solly cuts in,
A shot he did try,
Decent connection,
But goes left and high.

↓

26m: FANTASTIC SAVE BY KEPA

Great from Kaoru,
Mazy run and shot.
But can he finish?
He cannot.

↓

33m: KEPA SAVES, EVAN INJURED

A chance for Evan,
On the floor in pain.
Get subbed for Danny,
Such a shame.

↓

42m: DANNY WELBECK!!!!!!!!!!!! (1-1)

Well, it may be a shame,
But he's gone and scored!
Back post header,
Oh, my Lord!

↓

HALF-TIME RHYME

Look closely at the stats,
And I think you'll find.
Chelsea shouldn't be level,
They should be behind.

60m: ENCISO HITS THE POST!!

Great play from Julio,
Never say die.
Chased down the ball,
Danny's rebound goes high.

↓

65m: DOUBLE SANCHEZ SAVE

First, his right hand,
Then his knee.
For a second our defence,
Was all at sea.

↓

69m: TOP CORNER!! WHAT A GOOAAALLLL!!! (1-2)

JUST SENSATIONAL!!!
THE BALL WAS BLURRED!
JULIO FROM 30 YARDS,
WHAT HAS JUST OCCURRED??!!

↓

90m: MUDRYK SMASHES OVER

Mudryk tries to emulate,
What Julio did.
Ends up flying over,
(A smile, I hid.)

↓

90+8m: FINAL WHISTLE

What a feeling!!
What can we say?
We beat 'The Entitled',
Home and away.

Post-Match Ryhme

Next weekend we're back in London,
Heading down Wembley Way.
And after that performance,
It's hard to know what to say.

Evan out, Veltman too,
Frustrating and such a waste.
But to beat United, all we have to do,
Is take today and "cut & paste."

MATCH #37

Sunday, 23 April 2023

Manchester United 0 – 0 Brighton & Hove Albion AET (United win 7-6 on penalties.)

Competition: **The FA Cup - semi-final**
Kick-off: **16.30**
Venue: **Wembley Stadium, London**
Weather: **13c, dull**
Referee: **Craig Pawson**
Attendance: **81,445**

Squads

Manchester United: de Gea, Wan-Bissaka (Malacia 101), Lindelöf, Shaw, Dalot, Casemiro, Eriksen (Fred 62'), Antony (Sabitzer 90), Bruno Fernandes (Weghorst 101), Rashford, Martial (Sancho 85). **Unused subs:** Pellistri, Butland, Williams, Elanga.

Albion: Sanchez, Gross, Webster, Dunk, Estupinan, Caicedo, Enciso (Veltman 67), March, Mac Allister, Mitoma, Welbeck (Undav 72). **Unused subs:** Steele, Colwill, Ayari, Gilmour, van Hecke, Buonanotte, Offiah.

Match Preview

Living over 4500 miles away from Brighton, I don't get back to watch the Albion as much as I'd like to, but the chance to see us at Wembley against Manchester United was an opportunity I couldn't resist.

Having got up at 3am to secure one of the last few hundred tickets, as I lay in bed, my mind went back 40 years to when, as an 11-year-old, I watched the 1983 final on TV, which, having drawn 2-2, we went on to lose in the replay.

As I boarded my flight from Dallas to Heathrow a week later, there was only one thought on my mind — Revenge.

And I was hopeful, as with seven wins from our 13 Premier League games in 2023 (including a win at Old Trafford), our form heading into the game had put us in a great position to try and reach our first major cup final since our adventure 40 years ago.

We'd already seen off Middlesbrough, Liverpool, Stoke City and Grimsby Town, reaching the semi-finals for the first time since 2019. That day we lost 1-0 to Manchester City, but many felt that things could be very different this time.

Although United had lost both opening Premier League games, they had recovered well, with manager Erik ten Hag orchestrating a vast improvement. Despite being knocked out of the Europa League just a few days earlier by Seville, numerous players had returned to form, and the club were pushing for a Champions League spot.

However, our confidence was high following our emphatic 2-1 win at Stamford Bridge eight days earlier and with our head coach announcing that he had an entire squad to pick from, we also found ourselves in the somewhat unnerving position of being favourites.

AMERICAN
EXPRESS

Pre-Match Ryhme

37,000 seagulls head to Wembley,
Although some have had a rather large delay,
As London's packed, due to the fact,
The marathon's on the same day.

But I'm in my seat, Wembley's full,
What an atmosphere it creates.
Brighton fans are here from around the world,
Including this one from the United States.

In-Match Rhymes

1m: KICK-OFF

Evan is out,
Welbeck is in.
Here we go,
Man, what a din!

↓

7m: DE GEA SAVES FROM ALEXIS

Oh, my word,
That was close!
Right foot free-kick,
Pushed around the post.

↓

14m: SANCHEZ DENIES FERNANDEZ

Acres of space,
Decent shout.
Powerful shot,
Rob palms it out.

↓

17m: PERVIS FIRES OVER

What a chance!
Oh, what the heck.
Why didn't that fall,
To Welbeck?

↓

31m: ANOTHER CHANCE FOR US!

This time Enciso,
After a Mitoma run.
Right foot but wide,
Almost nil to one.

44m: INCHES WIDE FROM UNITED

Ball from the right,
Lands at Bruno's feet.
Amazing how both keepers,
Still have clean sheets.

↓

HALF-TIME RHYME

45 down,
45 to go.
I think there's going to be 30 more,
Following that, you know.

↓

50m: ESTUPINAN SENDS IT SAILING OVER

Solly's corner,
Dunk with a nod.
Lands at Pervis' feet,
High with his prod.

↓

57m: TIPPED OVER BY DE GEA

Julio our lad,
From Paraguay.
A right-foot rocket,
Wow, he let that one fly.

↓

57m: DANNY HEADS OVER

Corner comes in,
Super leap.
Over the bar,
I could weep.

64m: ANTONY'S EFFORT SAVED

The Brazilian shoots,
Sanchez's hands.
Are strong and steady,
All square as it stands.

↓

90m: NERVES

The whistle has gone,
I need some wine.
We're heading into,
Extra-time.

↓

94m: NO!! GREAT CHANCE FOR UNDAV!

Oh, Deniz!!!
He had no defenders near.
His first touch was poor,
And yet he was clear!

↓

105m: WORLD-CLASS FROM SANCHEZ

Rashford shoots,
Takes a deflection,
Superb save,
The ball changed direction.

↓

120m: PENALTY HEARTACHE

We were the better side,
I contends,
But by seven to six,
We go out on pens.

Post-Match Ryhme

After March's penalty flew over,
The rain soon began to fall.
So once Lindelof converted his,
I made a decent call.

I trudged back to Wembley Central,
And to ease the pain,
After heading back to the Sussex coast,
I drank as much beer as I could contain.

MATCH #38

Wednesday, 26 April 2023

Nottingham Forest 3 – 1 Brighton & Hove Albion

Competition: **Premier League**
Kick-off: **19.30**
Venue: **The City Ground, Nottingham**
Weather: **13c, clear skies**
Referee: **Jarred Gillett**
Attendance: **28,808**

Squads

Nottingham Forest: Navas, Williams (Kouyaté 65), Aurier, Niakhaté (Worrall 14), Felipe, Lodi, Danilo, Mangala, Gibbs-White, Johnson (Toffolo 86), Awoniyi (Ayew 80). **Unused subs:** Hennessey, Freuler, Lingard, Surridge, Dennis.

Albion: Steele, Gross, Dunk, Colwill, Estupinan (Welbeck 72), Mac Allister, Buonanotte (Offiah 88), March, Caicedo, Mitoma, Enciso (Undav 74). **Unused subs:** Sanchez, Veltman, Webster, Ayari, Gilmour, van Hecke.

Match Preview

I'd decided to stay in Brighton for a few days after the semi-final, so just three days after the Wembley heartache against Manchester United, I found myself watching the game in the Caxton Arms (a quaint Albion-themed pub in the centre of town) as we looked to bounce back against a struggling Nottingham Forest side for this midweek fixture at the City Ground.

Despite our Wembley disappointment, Albion still had plenty to play for as we targeted European football for the first time. Hopes of a top-six finish had been lifted with our 2-1 win over Chelsea last time out in the Premier League, and while we sat eighth, we had more games in hand than any other team.

Having not lost to a team currently sat in the bottom half of the table, we could have climbed to sixth depending on other results this week.

Steve Cooper's Forest team were battling for their top-tier status. Although they sat 19th before the game, a win would lift them out of the bottom three and up to 16th. However, the form table did not make good reading for Forest. Without a win since the beginning of February and on a four-game losing run, time was running out for them to secure their Premier League future.

Club news in the week had been dominated by the announcement that Evan Ferguson had signed a new long-term contract, and, as far as team news was concerned, De Zerbi had confirmed that Argentinian Facundo Buonanotte would make his first Premier League start.

AMERICAN EXPRESS
UNHCR
10
DANILO
28
AMERICAN EXPRESS
25
24

24
5
MAC ALLISTER
10
UNHCR
21
38

Pre-Match Ryhme

It's only three days since Wembley,
And I worry the lads won't be in their prime,
And that the mental impact of losing on penalties,
Means they could do with more downtime.

But tonight, we play a team with a glorious past,
Under Clough, European Cup winners twice.
And whilst a dominating 3-0 win would be ideal,
Honestly, a scrappy 1-0 will suffice.

In-Match Rhymes

1m: KICK-OFF

As the sun sets low,
In the sky,
Can fatigue,
The lads defy?

↓

6m: EVEN STEVENS

Forest having
To defend.
Although early chances,
At both ends.

↓

9m: PENALTY TO FOREST

Pervis hesitates,
Should have cleared.
Brings Williams down,
This is what we feared.

↓

11m: STEELE SAVES JOHNSON'S PENALTY!!!!!

Dives like Superman,
To his right,
Hit pretty well,
But perfect height.

↓

13m: CHANCE FOR FOREST

We don't clear our lines,
An act of folly.
Close from Danilo,
Blimey, what a volley!

16m: INCREDIBLE SAVE FROM NAVAS

I feel for Julio,
Forest relief.
His hands are on his hips,
In disbelief.

↓

33m: JOHNSON FIRES WIDE

What a chance,
Thankfully, Dunk is judged,
Only to have given him,
A 'little nudge'.

↓

38m: WE'RE AHEAD!!!! (0-1)

Robin Hood stole from the rich,
To give to the poor,
Facundo Buonanotte,
What a time to score!!!

↓

45+3m: FOREST HAVE AN EQUALISER (1-1)

A Pascal goal?
I'd usually revel.
But it's an OG,
Forest level.

↓

HALF-TIME RHYME

That was so unlucky,
I feel for Gross.
Jason almost saved it,
But I'm morose.

49m CLOSE FROM ESTUPINAN

Whilst Julio looks lively,
Forest look the better side.
Pervis has a shot from distance,
But unfortunately, it flies wide.

↓

58m: WASTEFUL FROM MITOMA

Brilliant from Buonanotte,
Kaoru through.
But his shot,
Went askew.

↓

68m: FOREST TAKE THE LEAD (2-1)

Moises lost possession,
In midfield,
But come on lads,
Their three points aren't sealed!

↓

90+1m: FOREST SCORE VIA ANOTHER PEN (3-1)

A Lewis handball,
Confirm VAR.
Their three points weren't sealed,
But now they are.

↓

90+13m: FINAL WHISTLE

I'm heading to bed,
Teeth are flossed.
Only positive?
Chelsea lost.

Post-Match Ryhme

There's a theme running through these poems,
Which is not a particularly healthy one, I fear.
And that's on the rare occasion that we lose a game,
I end up consuming way too much beer.

The lads tonight, they looked exhausted,
Whilst Forest fought for their lives.
So, as I sit in the pub, with beer and grub,
I don't think the result was a huge surprise.

MATCH #39

Saturday, 29 April 2023

Brighton & Hove Albion 6 – 0 Wolverhampton Wanderers

Competition: **Premier League**
Kick-off: **15.00**
Venue: **The Amex Stadium, Brighton**
Weather: **13c, sunny**
Referee: **David Coote**
Attendance: **31,584**

Squads

Albion: Steele, Veltman (Caicedo 64), Webster, Dunk, Estupinan, Gross, Gilmour, March (Mitoma 56), Enciso Mac Allister 64), Undav (Ayari 80), Welbeck (Buonanotte 56). **Unused subs:** Sanchez, Colwill, van Hecke, Offiah.

Wolves: Sa, Semedo (Podence 45), Dawson (Hwang 46), Kilman, Bueno (Toti 46), Lemina, Neves, Gomes, Nunes, Neto (Adama 82), Costa (Collins 45). **Unused subs:** Bentley, Moutinho, Sarabia, Cunha.

Match Preview

Whilst we had been playing plenty of football, the game against Wolves was our first Premier League home game since the beginning of the month.

Despite our loss to Nottingham Forest the previous Wednesday, our recent form was still strong. Only four teams had taken more points in the last eight Premier League games, with Roberto De Zerbi's men taking 14.

Our head coach had enjoyed his first away win as Albion boss against Wolves the previous November when Pascal Gross netted a late winner in a 3-2 victory at Molineux. Julen Lopetegui was unveiled as Wolves' new boss that day and had since guided them out of the relegation zone, and they were now eight points clear of the bottom three.

Our home support had seen us go unbeaten in our previous three Premier League games, having taken seven points. And, although victory would see us stay in eighth spot, we would close the gap between ourselves and Liverpool to just a point. On the other hand, a win for Wolves would see them move above Crystal Palace and Fulham into 11th.

In his pre-match press conference, whilst indicating that Adam Lallana may not play again this season and that Evan Ferguson was a doubt, De Zerbi confirmed that Joel Veltman was fit and would be in the starting lineup.

From a personal perspective, by way of a train, a coach, two planes and an Uber, I had completed the gruelling 21-hour trip from Brighton back to Tulsa via Charlotte and had only got to sleep a few hours earlier.

But I was up and ready.

AMERICAN EXPRESS
30
4

AstroPay
AMERICAN EXPRESS
AMERICAN EXPRESS
13

AMERICAN EXPRESS
UNIBET

Pre-Match Ryhme

The positive thing about flying west,
Is that the next day you spring out of bed.
So instead of snoozing with my wife,
I had breakfast at 6am instead.

We've now lost two games on the bounce,
And suddenly, regarding Europe, there are doubts.
So we're looking for a comprehensive win today,
If we're going to be getting our passports out.

In-Match Rhymes

1m: KICK-OFF

Warm and sunny here,
Looks the same there.
Rained when I was over,
Seems unfair.

↓

6m: UNDAV POKES HOME!!!!!! (1-0)

Quite low-key,
But he smiles with pride.
Once VAR confirms
That he's onside.

↓

13m: PASCAL. WHAT A MOVE!!! (2-0)

Gilmour to Julio,
Then to Gross.
Undav pulls defenders wide,
Grandiose!

↓

19m: WELBECK SHOULD MAKE IT THREE!

Their keeper falters,
As he tries to clear.
You'll get one, Danny,
Just persevere.

↓

24m: FABULOUS SAVE FROM STEELE

That was their first chance,
Since the match begun.
Thanks to Jason's right hand,
The score's not two-one.

26m: GROSS WITH HIS SECOND!! (3-0)

A stunning looping volley,
With his right peg.
Second assist from Julio,
Replay, I beg!

↓

39m: DANNY AT THE BACK POST!!! (4-0)

We cross to the back post,
For a reason.
Danny Welbeck is clinical,
At least his third this season?!

↓

45+3m: CLOSE FROM SOLLY

Nailing a half-volley,
Always hard.
Over the bar,
By at least a yard.

↓

HALF-TIME RHYME

Just fantastic,
Up by four.
And the way we're playing,
We could get four more!

↓

48m: IT'S FIVE!!! (5-0)

Seemed so simple,
Danny just swung his boot.
When we're in range,
The north stand shout "shoot"!

66m: DENIZ WITH HIS SECOND!!!! (6-0)

This one isn't set up,
By our Paraguayan.
Instead, it's a chip,
Undav's perfect nine iron.

↓

75m: GILMOUR DRAGS IT JUST WIDE

We're all over them,
In total control.
Billy inches away,
From his first Premier League goal.

↓

78m: STEELE FORCED INTO A SAVE

A cracking ball by Neves,
Splits open our defence.
Since he replaced Rob,
Jason's been immense.

↓

80m: WELL DONE DENIZ!

The home crowd show,
Their appreciation.
Bagged two goals,
And a standing ovation.

↓

90+2m: FINAL WHISTLE

Deniz, Pascal & Danny,
All get braces.
Wolves so poor,
Just not at the races.

Post-Match Ryhme

Some days things just seem to click,
And today was one of those.
Six of the best, on the pitch,
One of the season's best performances, I propose.

Spring sunshine at the Amex,
And a full house, what a sight.
It's Man United next, but if we play like that,
I think we'll do alright.

MATCH #40

Thursday, 4 May 2023

Brighton & Hove Albion 1 – 0 Manchester United

Competition: **Premier League**
Kick-off: **20.00**
Venue: **The Amex Stadium, Brighton**
Weather: **14c, sunshine & showers**
Referee: **Andre Marriner**
Attendance: **31,577**

Squads

Albion: Steele, Caicedo, Dunk, Webster, Estupinan, Mitoma, Mac Allister, Gilmour (Colwill 75), Buonanotte (March 62), Enciso, Welbeck (Undav 75). **Unused subs:** Sanchez, Ayari, van Hecke, Offiah, Moran, Peupion.

Manchester United: De Gea; Wan-Bissaka, Lindelof, Shaw, Dalot; Casemiro, Fred (Sabitzer 76); Antony (Sancho 76), Fernandes, Rashford; Martial (Weghorst 84). **Unused subs:** Butland, Maguire, Malacia, Williams, Eriksen, Pellistri.

Match Preview

Tonight's game marked the first of seven Premier League matches in May - the final push as we aimed to achieve our goal of European football for the 23/24 season. A win tonight would see us move up to sixth in the Premier League.

However, it was not an easy run-in, as five of those fixtures were against teams in the top seven. That included United, who sat fourth and could extend their lead over fifth-place Liverpool to ten points with a win.

Erik ten Hag's team also headed into the game knowing that they had got the better of us in the F.A. Cup semi-final just under a fortnight ago when they beat us on penalties to reach the final. That has been a part of a rich vein of form for United, who had won four of their last five Premier League games.

Roberto De Zerbi has confirmed that Joel Veltman was unlikely to be available, having been substituted against Wolves five days earlier and that Evan Ferguson would need to be assessed ahead of the game, having not featured in the Premier League since our 2-1 win over Chelsea on 15 April.

Now back in the U.S., I would rely on T.V. coverage for the rest of the season; it was a 14.00 kick-off for me for this memorable match.

Manchester, who?

STADIUM
TeamViewer

TeamViewer

Pre-Match Ryhme

For the second time in two weeks,
Manchester United are our foe.
Whilst we swap Wembley for the Amex,
Most of the same players are on show.

But for those heading up to Falmer,
In the perfect evening sun,
Create a din, as I predict we'll win,
By three goals to their one.

In-Match Rhymes

1m: KICK-OFF

Games in hand,
And currently 8th.
Trust Roberto,
And keep the faith.

↓

2m: HUGE CHANCE FOR UNITED

What a chance,
Early doors.
Anthony through,
Almost scores.

↓

4m: MITOMA DENIED

He's one-on-one,
With de Gea,
Couldn't finish,
But what a player.

↓

13m: CLOSE AGAIN FROM MITOMA

A few minutes ago,
de Gea denied.
Now he cuts in from the left,
And strikes one wide.

↓

28m: STEELE DENIES RASHFORD

The away support,
Making noises.
Rashford drops his shoulder,
And goes straight past Moises.

37m: ENCISO DRIVES WIDE

Good advantage played,
By the man in black.
Decent effort,
After a swift attack.

↓

45m: BUONANOTTE GOES CLOSE

Every time he plays,
You can see his confidence grow.
And that left-foot curler,
Wasn't far away, you know.

↓

HALF-TIME RHYME

We're great in possession,
And luckily Jason's awake.
Both sides have had chances,
Please, just one can we take?

↓

58m: CHANCES FOR ALBION

Incredibly, at the Amex,
We're still level pegging.
Kaoru then Danny,
Two chances go begging.

↓

69m: ANTHONY HACKS DOWN MAC ALLISTER

The Brazilian's gone ballistic,
Completely losing his cool.
Now tries to square up to Lewis,
Oh, what a fool.

70m: HEY, PGMOL

Instead of an apology,
Can you give the rules a tweak,
And put us two ahead,
Using one of our six from last week?

↓

90m: GREAT SAVE BY DE GEA

What a strike by Alexis!!
But in this little rhyme,
I say we stay optimistic,
As there's loads of added time

↓

90+7m: OMG!! HANDBALL!!! PENALTY TO US!!!!!

At the Amex, we were heading,
For a draw, when.
Luke Shaw's arm hit the ball,
And VAR has said it's a pen!!!!!

↓

90+9m: GOOOOAAALLLLLLLL!!!!!!!!!!!! (1-0)

I've just woken the dead,
With how loud I did shout.
Alexis vs. de Gea,
IT WAS NEVER IN DOUBT!!!

↓

90+10m: FINAL WHISTLE

If only you could see,
The size of my grin.
There's just nothing like,
A LAST-MINUTE WIN!!!!

Post-Match Ryhme

It's all over at the AMEX!
The final whistle, it just blew,
And I'm finding typing as I'm shouting,
A very hard thing to do!

A 1-0 win with a last-minute penalty,
It honestly could have been more,
And whilst Maradona thanked the 'Hand of God',
We thank the 'Hand of Shaw'.

MATCH #41

Monday, 8 May 2023

Brighton & Hove Albion 1 – 5 Everton

Competition: **Premier League**
Kick-off: **17.30**
Venue: **The Amex Stadium, Brighton**
Weather: **12c, drizzle**
Referee: **Simon Hooper**
Attendance: **31,567**

Squads

Albion: Steele, Gross, Webster (Colwill 45), Dunk, Estupinan, Caicedo, Mac Allister, Buonanotte (March 45 (Gilmour 77)), Mitoma, Undav (Enciso 45), Welbeck (Ferguson 45). **Unused subs:** Sanchez, Ayari, van Hecke, Moran.

Everton: Pickford, Patterson, Mina, Tarkowski, Mykolenko, Garner, Gueye (Onana 87), Iwobi, Doucouré, McNeil, Calvert-Lewin, (Maupay 87). **Unused subs:** Holgate, Keane, Gray, Begovic, Davies, Coady, Simms

Match Preview

The King's coronation and our crowded fixture schedule meant we headed to the Amex on a damp Bank Holiday afternoon for our fifth game in 16 days. However, following our 99th-minute winner against Manchester United just a few days earlier, anticipation was high that we could secure our third consecutive home win.

Victory would mean our sixth Premier League double of the season, having won 4-1 at Goodison Park on 3 January, and would lift us to sixth in the table and keep our push for European football on track.

Whilst Jakub Moder, Adam Lallana and Tariq Lamptey remained long-term absentees, head coach Roberto De Zerbi had indicated that there was a chance that Evan Ferguson, who scored when the teams met at Goodison Park, could return after missing four games with an ankle injury. Joel Veltman was also a doubt, having missed last Thursday's win over Manchester United with a hamstring injury.

Everton had just as much to play for. Three points could lift them from 19th to 16th as they battled for top-flight survival under Sean Dyche, who had replaced Frank Lampard as head coach earlier in the year.

AMERICAN EXPRESS
Stake.com
13
27
16

Stake.com
AMERICAN EXPRESS
17
22
5
13
10
27
DOUCOURE
16
20
37
bet365

Pre-Match Ryhme

I'm typing this at the gym again,
Confused as to why my weight is staying the same.
Anyway, I'm jumping in the truck to drive,
Back home to watch the game.

My concern about Everton is their manager,
As Sean Dyche represents a bitter pill.
Last year when he was in charge of Burnley,
I flew back and watched them thrash us three to nil.

In-Match Rhymes

1m: KICK-OFF

Bright colours at the Amex
Made me blink.
Us, blue & white,
Everton, pink.

↓

1m: EVERTON SCORE. (0-1)

Total meltdown,
On Twitter beckons.
Doucoure scores,
After 34 seconds!

↓

10m: WHAT'S GOING ON?

I can't believe we're behind,
Usually, we'd be content.
As when it comes to possession,
We're at 90%.

↓

15m: WORRYING

This is unexpected,
And ain't much fun.
15 gone,
Already squeaky bum.

↓

20m: UNFORCED ERRORS

We're looking oddly,
Off the pace.
Second ball.
Second place.

26m: TREMENDOUS BLOCKS

Gross and Webster,
Just immense.
10 yards out,
Great defence

↓

29m: DOUCOURE DOUBLES EVERTON'S LEAD (0-2)

Everton attack with speed,
On the break,
Come on lads,
Give your heads a shake!

↓

35m: THIS CAN'T BE HAPPENING!! (0-3)

A low-driven cross,
Surely, we now can't win,
Unlucky Steele,
Goes in off his shin. (OG)

↓

HALF-TIME RHYME

Three nil down,
I already need a drink.
It seems there are more players,
Wearing pink.

↓

46m: HALF-TIME CHANGES FOR ALBION

Some Albion fans already,
Heading for the pubs?
Roberto makes,
Four half-time subs.

59m: CLOSE FROM EVAN

Oh, so close,
Ferguson denied.
Header saved by Pickford,
Oh, offside.

↓

76m: MCNEIL SCORES FOR EVERTON (0-4)

On the break again,
Just uncanny.
(And whilst chasing back,
Solly's now done his hammy.)

↓

79m: MAC ALLISTER PULLS ONE BACK (1-4)

I still have hope,
Rather than expectation.
Off Alexis's shoulder,
For a consolation.

↓

90+6m: MCNEIL ADDS A FIFTH (1-5)

It pains me to say it,
Everton, take a bow.
They think it's all over
Well, it is now.

↓

90+8m: FINAL WHISTLE

As the drizzle falls,
I'm off to brood.
Have to say,
Dyche was shrewd.

Post-Match Ryhme

The club's website has it right,
No doubt a night we should forget.
Hated getting beaten,
Bet you hated getting wet.

The boys looked tired, and it's been tough,
Their fifth game in 16 days.
So, I, for one, won't be criticising,
This most unexpected of displays.

MATCH #42

Sunday, 14 May 2023

Arsenal 0 – 3 Brighton & Hove Albion

Competition: **Premier League**
Kick-off: **16.30**
Venue: **The Emirates Stadium, London**
Weather: **13c, partly sunny**
Referee: **Andy Madley**
Attendance: **60,139**

Squads

Arsenal: Ramsdale, White, Kiwior, dos Santos Magalhães, Tierney, Ødegaard (Smith-Rowe 77), Jorginho (Partey 60), Xhaka (Nelson 60), Saka, Jesus (Nketiah 77), Martinelli (Trossard 20). **Unused subs:** Holding, Vieira, Turner, Walters.

Albion: Steele, Gross, Dunk, Colwill, Estupinan, Mac Allister, Caicedo, Enciso (Undav 82), Mitoma, Gilmour (Welbeck 61), Ferguson (Bounoanotte 77). **Unused subs:** McGill, Ayari, van Hecke, Offiah, Moran, Peupion.

Match Preview

Whilst I know social media isn't necessarily an accurate barometer of fans' feelings, I had taken a break from it following the loss to Everton the previous Monday. Too many people seemed full of doom and gloom and predicting the end of our European hopes, forgetting it was our first home defeat in six and that we had enjoyed four wins in our previous six Premier League matches.

These had included victories on the road at Bournemouth and Chelsea, which had helped us pass our record points total in the top-flight with five games still to play – we were currently on 55, four better off than our final total last season.

While our away form had been impressive, with seven wins from 16 games on the road, we knew it would take something special to take points off Arsenal at the Emirates.

Only Manchester City (49) and Liverpool (43) had taken more points at home this season than the Gunners (42), with both north-west sides having played a game more.

Whilst a win would see us move to sixth place, it would all but end the Gunners' title ambitions which had been slowly slipping away in recent weeks.

As far as injuries were concerned, the news was mixed. Whilst De Zerbi was able to confirm that striker Evan Ferguson was available again, unfortunately, Adam Webster and Solly March wouldn't be, with the latter having apparently pulled a hamstring in the game against Everton.

It was raining cats and dogs in Tulsa, and a storm was brewing at the Emirates, too.

AMERICAN EXPRESS
28
AMERICAN EXPRESS
25

RAMSDALE
1
Emirates
FLY BETTER
AMERICAN EXPRESS

Pre-Match Ryhme

Some say that after a setback,
And if you want to come back stronger.
You should 'get back on the bike' straight away,
As it's not ideal to wait too much longer.

Whilst our loss to Everton was a setback,
We're into the last few games of the season.
Let's stand together and support the lads,
As any pessimism has no rhyme or reason.

In-Match Rhymes

1m: KICK-OFF

Here we go,
All aboard,
As we put Arsenal's title ambitions.
To the sword.

↓

5m: MITOMA FLOORED BY MARTINELLI!!

Not even a card?
It was clear to see.
More like a wrestling move,
If you ask me.

↓

12m: STEELE GIVING ME A HEART ATTACK

Playing it out from the back,
Is what we do,
But that was nearly intercepted,
A collective "phew"!

↓

24m: STEELE DENIES JESUS AT HIS NEAR POST

Lost the ball,
Arsenal quick to break,
Playing this way,
Chances we'll take.

↓

30m: GOOD STATISTICS

Not a flowing game,
That's my impression,
But we're having more of the ball,
66% possession.

31m: CLOSE FOR ARSENAL!

Having come on for Martinelli,
Trossard hits the bar.
Seeing him in red & white,
Still feels bizarre.

↓

37m: CHANCE FOR ENCISO

Mitoma skins Ben White,
On the wing,
Julio fires over,
To hope, I cling.

↓

45+2m: JUST WIDE FROM SAKA!

If I could've hit a pause button,
I would have bet,
That was destined for,
The back of the net.

↓

HALF-TIME RHYME

Quality play,
Has been rare,
First 45?
Messy affair.

↓

51m: GOALLLLL!! ENCISO HEADER!!! (0-1)

A long ball from Levi,
Mitoma beats White for pace.
Crossed in by Pervis,
The boys embrace!!

65m: ARTETA BOOKED

With the fourth official,
A few choice words he shares,
You have to keep your head, Mikel,
When all about you are losing theirs.

↓

80m: SLOWING THINGS DOWN

We're not naive,
And so it starts.
At least we're learning,
The dark arts.

↓

86m: UNDAV PUTS US TWO UP!!!! (0-2)

Great lob from Deniz,
Title dreams dismissed.
And none other than Trossard,
With the assist!!

↓

90+6m PERVISSSSSSSS!! (0-3)

The first goal of the season,
For our Ecuadorian star,
(Would have been his second,
Had it not been for VAR.)

↓

90+8m: FINAL WHISTLE

Bloody hell!
Three nil away.
What team,
WHAT A DAY!!!!

Post-Match Ryhme

His name is Kaoru Mitoma,
And he doesn't wish to boast,
But he won't need to eat tonight,
As he's just enjoyed Ben White on toast.

What an all-round performance,
From the team in blue & white.
I know you put them away last week,
But you can get your passports out again tonight.

MATCH #43

Thursday, 18 May 2023

Newcastle United 4 – 1 Brighton & Hove Albion

Competition: **Premier League**
Kick-off: **19.30**
Venue: **St. James' Park, Newcastle**
Weather: **15c, partly sunny**
Referee: **Robert Jones**
Attendance: **52,122**

Squads

Newcastle United: Pope, Trippier (Targett 95), Schär, Botman, Burn, Willock (Anderson 61), Guimarães Rodriguez Moura, Joelinton (Manquillo 95), Almirón (Saint-Maximin 94), Wilson, Isak (Gordon 94). **Unused subs:** Dubravka, Dummett, Lewis, Miley.

Albion: Steele, Caicedo, Dunk, van Hecke, Estupinan, Gilmour (Mac Allister 56), Gross (Offiah 69), Mitoma, Welbeck (Ferguson 56), Undav (Peupion 85), Buonanotte (Enciso 56). **Unused subs:** McGill, Ayari, Peupion, Samuels.

Match Preview

The games were coming thick and fast, and whilst many had rightfully raised the question of how the punishing schedule would affect the players, I was equally concerned about us supporters. I, for one, was shattered!

We headed north-east in search of three points that would see us take a huge step towards qualifying for European football for the first time.

Our 3-0 win over Arsenal on Sunday (our fifth win from our last eight league matches and our eighth win on the road this season) meant we now needed just two wins from our remaining four games to secure sixth spot and Europa League football at the Amex for the 23/24 season.

However, the game was just as crucial for Newcastle, who needed two wins to confirm their spot in next season's Champions League. It had been an incredible season for Eddie Howe's men, who, after winning just one of their opening seven league games, had gone on impressive winning runs to propel themselves into third spot with three games to play.

Unfortunately, the long season had begun to take its toll on our squad, with Roberto De Zerbi confirming that Joel Veltman, Adam Webster and Solly March were all unavailable.

Goalkeeper Robert Sanchez was also not in the squad, but it was thought this was not injury-related.

AMERICAN EXPRESS
FFICIAL BETTING
AMERICAN EXPRESS
27

AMERICAN
EXPRESS
PARI MATCH

Pre-Match Ryhme

We currently lie in sixth place,
With a game or two still in hand.
As we head up to north-east England,
And arguably the wealthiest club in the land.

Could a club that's owned by a country,
Be beaten by a stony 'beach'?
In the words of Kevin Keegan, "I'd just love it" if,
A footballing lesson we could teach.

In-Match Rhymes

1m: KICK-OFF

Necessary innovation,
Means squad rotation.
Punishing schedule,
Is the causation.

↓

6m: SHOT BLOCKED BY VAN HECKE

Almiron shoots,
Just lacked poise.
Man, the Geordies,
I can't believe the noise.

↓

8m: DUNK CLEARS FROM JUST OFF THE LINE

A cross from Isak,
And although the touch was thin.
It came off Caicedo,
And was heading in.

↓

22m: CAPTAIN FANTASTIC

We were too sloppy,
At the back,
But Dunk's outstretched leg,
Nullifies the attack.

↓

22m: NEWCASTLE AHEAD FROM A CORNER [1-0]

That, Deniz Undav,
You did not intend.
He's just scored again,
But at the wrong end.

30m: VAR CHECK FOR NEWCASTLE PENALTY

Such great acting,
Wilson could be in Othello.
Newcastle striker lucky,
Not to receive a yellow.

↓

37m: MITOMA CURLS ONE OVER

He's had a quiet half,
But then cuts in.
Shoots wide from distance,
His face, chagrin.

↓

45+4m: BURN DOUBLES NEWCASTLE'S LEAD [2-0]

We know he's 7ft 3,
As he played for us.
And from a free kick,
So dangerous.

↓

HALF-TIME RHYME

What a time,
To let them score,
I'd better not type the word,
I'm looking for!

↓

50m: BRILLIANT STOP BY STEELE

That's world-class,
Super save.
Consequences of conceding,
Would have been grave.

51m: GOAL!!! DENIZ!!!!!!! [2-1]

He didn't have the best half,
Thought he was down and out.
Great ball from Gilmour,
Back in with a shout!

↓

65m: KITCHEN SINK!

Saves, blocks, headers,
We finally get it clear.
It's like a ball in a pinball machine,
On the pier.

↓

69m: ENCISO NODS JUST WIDE

We've been the better side,
In the second half.
But that will count for nowt,
On the game's epitaph.

↓

89m & 90+1M: NEWCASTLE SCORE TWO IN TWO

Finely balanced,
But not our day.
Two chances created,
Both put away.

↓

90+9m: FINAL WHISTLE

It's all over,
The lads are fatigued.
But I'm still predicting,
The Europa League.

Post-Match Ryhme

We've yet another game on Sunday,
Does it ever end?
Our games in hand were cards up our sleeve,
But now they're not our friend.

In the first half, we were disjointed,
And could honestly have been down by more.
But hats off, Newcastle, you played well,
And deserve your place in the top four.

MATCH #44

Sunday, 21 May 2023

Brighton & Hove Albion 3 – 1 Southampton

Competition: **Premier League**
Kick-off: **14.00**
Venue: **The Amex Stadium, Brighton**
Weather: **19c, scattered clouds**
Referee: **Paul Tierney**
Attendance: **31,507**

Squads

Albion: Steele, Veltman (Undav 74), Dunk, Colwill (van Hecke 89), Estupinan, Caicedo, Gross, Mitoma (Gilmour 89), Mac Allister, Ferguson (Welbeck 65), Enciso (Bounanotte 45). **Unused subs:** McGill, Ayari, Moran, Peupion.

Southampton: McCarthy, Bree (Livramento 77), Bednarek, Lyanco, Walker-Peters, Lavia (Doyle 84), Ward-Prowse, Elyounoussi (Kamaldeen 71), Alcaraz (S Armstrong 71), Walcott, Aribo (Ballard 70). **Unused subs:** Bazunu, Ćaleta-Car, Maitland-Niles, Onuachu.

Match Preview

Despite our 4-1 defeat to Newcastle three days earlier, Albion's European hopes were still very much in our hands as we entered our penultimate home game of the Premier League season.

Two wins from our final three games would see us secure sixth place and Europa League football, while a win today would guarantee at least Europa Conference League football.

Southampton had been the first club to have had their relegation confirmed, and with just a point taken in their last eight games, Ruben Selles's side were rooted to the bottom of the table with 24 points from 36 games.

Roberto De Zerbi had confirmed that Joel Veltman was available after recovering from a hamstring injury, and Levi Colwill was back in the squad, too. Adam Webster was still out, but Albion had no fresh injury worries after Thursday's game at Newcastle.

The day after our loss to Newcastle, I'd flown to Germany for work and had serious doubts about whether I'd be able to watch this crucial match. However, having convinced Hans, the manager of O'Reilly's Irish pub next to Frankfurt Railway Station, to donate the smallest of his numerous TV screens to show it, I was all set.

Memories of the next few hours are impacted by the effects of too many German beers, but as I stumbled back to my hotel 10 hours after the final whistle, I was still smiling following this momentous afternoon.

AMERICAN EXPRESS
AMERICAN EXPRESS
10
FERGUSON
28
JOIN
G
STEELE
23

CAICEDO
25
22
GROSS
13
MAC ALLISTER
10
AMERICAN EXPRESS

Pre-Match Ryhme

Finally, we've had a bit of luck,
As yesterday's results seemed to go our way.
And we're especially grateful to Brentford,
Who, against Spurs, put on a great display.

Aston Villa dropped points too,
Meaning we Seagulls can raise a toast.
As if we can win at the Amex today,
Of at least the Europa Conference League, we can boast.

In-Match Rhymes

1m: KICK-OFF

21st of May,
2023.
Here we go,
Let's make history.

↓

4m: SOLID START

Easy does it,
We're exercising discretion.
But looking so comfortable,
In possession.

↓

8m: GREAT CHANCE FOR MITOMA!

He created space,
At the edge of the box.
Fires it wide,
The Amex rocks.

↓

17m: HUGE CHANCE FOR SOUTHAMPTON

Our defence exposed,
As Southampton break.
Luckily the opportunity,
Alcaraz can't take.

↓

22m: MITOMA HITS THE POST

When it comes to goals,
He could have so many more,
Oh, Kaoru,
You HAVE to score.

28m: SQUEAKY BUM

The defender took it,
Off Pervis' toes.
This game already feels,
Like "one of those".

↓

29m: BOOOOOOOMMMMMMM!!!!! (1-0)

At the edge of the box,
He's given acres of spaces.
Evan with a missile,
Right off his laces!!

↓

40m: EVAN STRIKES AGAIN!!! (2-0)

Put on a plate,
For him to shoot,
By a world-class ball,
From Mitoma's right boot.

↓

45+3m: MITOMA SENDS IT INTO THE SIDE NETTING

Once he opens his dribbling,
Box of tricks.
He creates so many chances,
He could have six!

↓

HALF-TIME RHYME

We are almost in Europe,
And are all feeling merry.
It's like being 45min from Dieppe,
If we were going by ferry.

58m: SOUTHAMPTON PULL ONE BACK (2-1)

Bound to happen.
Guaranteed.
Just what my heart,
Didn't need.

↓

62m: SAINTS EQUALISER RULED OUT

Oh, my word,
Just for a minute,
I thought we'd let,
Saints back in it.

↓

68m: VELTMAN GOES CLOSE

Drilled free kick from Gross,
Header from Joel.
Only a superb save,
Denies a goal.

↓

69m: GRRROOOOOOOOSSSSSSSSSSSSSSS!!! (3-1)

Bottom right-hand corner,
What's the worry?!
Now our joint highest scorer,
With Maupay and Murray!

↓

90+7m: FINAL WHISTLE

I've tried to remove it,
But no matter how hard I try.
There seems to be something,
In my eye.

Post-Match Ryhme

The beers are flowing, the tears too,
It's hard to know what to say.
Weeping in front of a group of strangers,
Some just shook their head and looked away.

But I am not in the least embarrassed,
As we've never got to say this in the past.
As next season, its passports out,
"WE'RE GOING ON A EUROPEAN TOUR AT LAST!!!!!"

MATCH #45

Wednesday, 24 May 2023

Brighton & Hove Albion 1 – 1 Manchester City

Competition: **Premier League**
Kick-off: **20.00**
Venue: **The Amex Stadium, Brighton**
Weather: **16c, partly cloudy**
Referee: **Simon Hooper**
Attendance: **31,388**

Squads

Albion: Steele, Gross, van Hecke, Colwill, Estupinan, Gilmour (Mac Allister 51), Caicedo, Buonanotte (Veltman 75), Welbeck (Undav 75), Enciso (Ferguson 51), Mitoma. **Unused subs:** McGill, Webster, Dunk, Ayari, Peupion.

Manchester City: Ortega Moreno, Walker, Stones (Gomez 84), Rodrigo, Lewis, Gundogan (C), De Bruyne (Alvarez 57), Bernardo (Phillips 84), Mahrez, Foden (Palmer 51), Haaland. **Unused subs:** Ederson, Charles, O'Reilly, Robertson, Knight.

Match Preview

Albion looked to secure the point we needed to guarantee Europa League football next season via this highly anticipated Wednesday night game.

Our 3-1 victory over Southampton on Sunday confirmed that we would be participating in European competition for the first time in our history, with at least seventh spot secured.

While it would take a substantial goal difference swing in Albion's last two games to see us drop from sixth to seventh, our aim was to ensure that there was nothing riding on our last game of the season at Villa Park a few days later.

A run of six wins in our last ten outings has seen us over the line, but City's form was hugely impressive too.

They had dropped just two points in a 15-game unbeaten run that had seen them snatch the title out of Arsenal's hands — a run that saw them beat the Gunners twice, as well as the likes of Liverpool and Newcastle.

With the Premier League title in the bag, Pep Guardiola's men had the treble in their sights as the Champions League final against Inter Milan would follow the FA Cup final against rivals Manchester United.

Unfortunately, I was attending a gala-dinner event in Frankfurt, but I knew it would be over just before kick-off. It was, therefore, with great relief that I was able to join other seagulls crowded around a tiny iPhone to watch the match as 700 people danced the night away around us.

MITOMA
22

Pre-Match Ryhme

The champions are coming to the Amex,
At the weekend, they won the league.
After Arsenal lost to Forest,
So as to Pep's line-up, I am intrigued.

I don't care if Haaland gets a hat-trick,
As long as we score the same as them or more.
And as every seagull will be keen to tell you,
We've beaten them here before.

In-Match Rhymes

1m: KICK-OFF

Only just sat down,
Have seen the side.
I'm watching on a screen,
Four inches wide.

↓

5m: HAALAND WITH TWO CHANCES

A close header,
A bicycle kick.
Didn't connect properly,
But nice trick.

↓

17m: GROSS EFFORT SAVED.

Julio was tripped,
A free kick is the result.
Pascal has a go,
After he and Moises consult.

↓

20m: WELBECK HITS THE CROSSBAR

Another free kick,
This time a bit nearer.
It's a great strike,
But it's no Alan Shearer.

↓

22m: HAALAND THROUGH ON GOAL

I honestly thought,
We'd go behind.
But he had a heavy touch,
Which I don't mind.

25m: FODEN PUTS CITY IN FRONT (1-0)

Foden to Haaland,
"Give it here".
van Hecke on the line,
But he can't clear.

↓

31m: MITOMA HAS GOAL RULED OUT

From Pascal's corner,
What a din.
But, yes, on replay,
He pushed it in.

↓

38m: OH, MY WORD!!!!!!! JULIO ENCISO!!!!!!! (1-1)

HIS GOAL AGAINST CHELSEA,
I THOUGHT NO ONE BETTERS!
BUT I THINK HE JUST HAS,
HENCE THE CAPITAL LETTERS!!

↓

40m: WOW. JUST WOW!!

Julio's 30-yard strike,
Deserves another rhyme.
And the lad is yet,
To reach his prime

↓

44m: WELBECK SCORES - BUT IT'S OFFSIDE

A brilliant finish,
But there is a snag.
The lino's outstretched arm,
Holding a flag.

45m: FODEN'S HEADER GRAZES THE BAR

You just can't switch off,
For a minute.
But they are the Champions,
So that's obvious, innit?

↓

HALF-TIME RHYME

What entertainment,
The Amex rocking!
At the Europa League's door,
We are knocking.

↓

76m: JUST WIDE FROM ESTUPINAN

To say it could be 4-1,
May sound folly.
Mitoma and Evan go close,
Followed by a Pervis left-foot volley.

↓

80m: HAALAND GOAL RULED OUT

A Palmer cross,
He did convert.
But there's a clear pull,
On Colwill's shirt.

↓

90+5m: FINAL WHISTLE

Mitoma could have won it,
After their goal was disallowed.
But it ends honours even,
Man, I'm oh, so proud.

Post-Match Ryhme

We did it! What an achievement!
Never been so happy with a one-all draw.
And as for Julio Encisco,
What a way to score!

We're going to play in the Europa League,
Surreal right now, it seems.
And I'm an optimist and expect great things,
But never in my wildest dreams..!

MATCH #46

Sunday, 28 May 2023

Aston Villa 2 – 1 Brighton & Hove Albion

Competition: **Premier League**
Kick-off: **16.30**
Venue: **Villa Park, Birmingham**
Weather: **18c, bright**
Referee: **David Coote**
Attendance: **42,212**

Squads

Aston Villa: Martínez, Cash, Konsa, Mings, Digne, Kamara, Douglas Luiz, Bailey (Buendía 69'), McGinn, Ramsey, Watkins. **Unused subs:** Diego Carlos, Traoré, Chambers, Ashley Young, Olsen, Dendoncker, Revan, Patterson.

Albion: Steele, Veltman (Estupinan 45), Webster (van Hecke 65), Colwill, Buonanotte, Gross, Mac Allister, Ayari (Caicedo 45), Enciso (Mitoma 65), Ferguson, Undav (Hinshelwood 89). **Unused subs:** McGill, Dunk, Welbeck, Gilmour.

Match Preview

And so, after a momentous and historic season, the end of the road had finally arrived.

Four days earlier, our 1-1 draw with Manchester City confirmed our sixth-place finish and a Europa League spot.

Albion were now 11 points better off than in any other top-flight campaign in the club's history, with our away form a significant contributor. Our 28 points on the road was the fourth-best record in the Premier League this season. However, Villa needed to match Tottenham's result against Leeds to ensure they finished in the Europa Conference League in seventh position, and we knew we had a job on our hands to add another three points to that tally.

Unai Emery's men not only wanted to secure European football but were also aiming to do the double over us, which only two other teams had achieved this year.

Whilst we were hopeful of having Adam Webster and Joel Veltman available, I was pleased there was nothing huge riding on the game for us. Villa had undergone a resurgence following the appointment of Emery and were now a challenging prospect – especially at Villa Park and with their eyes on Europe.

AMERICAN EXPRESS
STOPS
13
CAICEDO
25
WATKINS
11

AMERICAN EXPRESS
CAZOO
Search. Drive. Smile.

Pre-Match Ryhme

I expect if Villa teak the lead,
Martinez will try to play the fool.
Has a history of doing so,
It would seem he thinks it's cool.

Cramp will hit their players,
Time-wasting? Oh, for sure.
But I ain't caring, as we're declaring,
We're going on a EUROPEAN TOUR!

In-Match Rhymes

1m: KICK-OFF

On a European journey,
Will we both embark?
An electric atmosphere,
At Villa Park.

↓

2m: PLAYING IT OUT AT THE BACK

I like that we try it,
Week after week.
But my heart doesn't enjoy it,
Is my only critique.

↓

4m: BAILEY HITS THE CROSSBAR

Cross came in,
Good first touch.
Just stayed out,
But not by much.

↓

8m: LUIZ PUTS VILLA IN FRONT (1-0)

Such a simple goal,
Loads of space.
Ramsey cuts it back,
Side-foot and placed.

↓

9m: OVER THE BAR FROM FERGUSON

What a ball from Alexis,
Evan onside.
Strikes one from distance,
In his stride.

20m: UNDAV'S GOAL DISALLOWED

It seems to have happened,
Far too many times.
Julio offside,
Once VAR has drawn the lines.

↓

26m: WATKINS DOUBLES VILLA'S LEAD (2-0)

The only lines now are stud marks,
Down Alexis' ankle.
Surely fouled in the build-up?
We are rankled.

↓

30m: FERGUSON DENIED BY KAMARA

He's through on goal again,
Past the last man.
But can the defender get a leg in?
Yes, he can.

↓

38m: UNDAV...AND THIS TIME, IT STANDS!!! (2-1)

Offside from the free kick,
The lino's given.
But the VAR overturns,
The on-field decision.

↓

45m: GREAT CHANCE FOR AN EQUALISER!!

Undav having his best game,
In an Albion shirt.
Martinez spreads himself wide,
Deniz can't convert.

HALF-TIME RHYME

Behind at Villa,
So frustrating.
But on thin ice,
They are skating,

↓

55m: PERVIS & MOISES ON

They were half-time subs,
Into the side.
The former sets him up,
But Alexis smacks it wide.

↓

57m: RAMSEY MISSES A SITTER

From five yards
He's managed to send.
The ball into row Z,
Of the Holte end.

↓

90+5m: BRILLIANT KEEPING FROM STEELE

With only one goal in it,
It was always tight,
Will they make the Conference League?
I think they might.

↓

90+6m: FINAL WHISTLE

Both sides in Europe,
Bring out the beers.
So hard to see,
Alexis in tears.

Post-Match Ryhme

Congratulations, Aston Villa,
You'll play in Europe too.
(Even though I must point out,
We're in a higher league than you,)

You certainly have decent fans,
And because I need to make it rhyme.
Your team also have many skills,
The most efficient being wasting time. :)

ABOUT THE BRIGHTON BARD

Have you ever tried to fully comprehend the multitude of tiny, seemingly innocuous life events that lead you to exactly where you are today?

Careers, relationships and ultimately whole lives can be transformed by 'sliding door' moments, most of which we have no control over.

One of my biggest 'sliding door' moments occurred in May 1983.

Yes, an iconic date in Brighton & Hove Albion's history was also one that became a pivotal moment in my young life. I had just turned 11 when my dad got a new job in Sussex, and the whole family uprooted from the outskirts of Birmingham and moved to Horsham.

I often think of where I'd be if my dad hadn't got the job.

Certainly not living in America. And maybe not even a fan of the Albion.

Already football mad, I joined a youth side called Roffey Robins for the '83/'84 season and thus embarked on a journey which led to me representing numerous clubs at various levels of Sussex football.

After three seasons with Roffey Robins, I joined Horsham Sparrows at under 15 level and, a few months into my second season, got invited for trials for the soon-to-be-launched Horsham F.C. youth side in 1988. The team was managed by Andy, Tony & Franco Massimo — the latter played for Brighton at reserve level, I believe — and these three charismatic brothers went on to have a huge and positive impact on my footballing life as they managed a number of us who went on to represent both Horsham F.C. and Horsham YMCA at senior level, too.

In 1990, aged 18 and having just about scraped three A-levels, another pivotal moment was deciding to apply to study at the old Brighton Polytechnic in Falmer instead of somewhere further afield. The course was called 'Media & Information' (whatever that meant), and the main classroom was just a few meters from where the Amex now sits. I used to park my

little Renault 5 approximately where the club store is, and, whilst quite a few of the original buildings got demolished when the Amex was built, I can still make out one of our classrooms through the fence opposite Dick's bar when I make it back for a home game.

While studying at the Poly, I represented Cowfold FC in the West Sussex League and then Storrington in the County League, the latter managed by the aforementioned Massimos, who led us to promotion to County League Two in 1993.

Having completed my degree at what had become Brighton University in June 1993, I got my first job in September and, having spent two enjoyable seasons with Steyning F.C. under Alf Ford, achieved my highest standard of football in the mid-90s when I played for Lewes FC for a couple of seasons in the Rymans League under Terry Parris.

Although I have lived in Brighton, I spent most of my 30+ years in the city living in Hove and, at one point, lived in Hartington Villas, where the floodlights of the Goldstone would light up the back garden. However, midweek training and Saturday games meant I didn't watch the Albion play live until the mid-2000s. My earliest memories are, therefore, the occasional game at the Withdean and a trip to the Millennium Stadium for the 2004 League Two playoff final. I didn't secure a season ticket until we reached the Amex in 2011.

Fast forward a few years, and I met my wife Melissa whilst working in Argentina in 2015, was married in 2019 and now live on the edge of the Great Plains of Oklahoma whilst running my own small business, enjoying watching the Albion from afar and, of course, writing the occasional rhyme!

I'm not yet sure whether I'll be able to afford the time to do another of these books for the 23/24 season. What I do know is that I'll still be regularly sharing short poems on social media and have some other ideas in the pipeline. So, if you want to stay connected and would enjoy some more content like this, find me via @TheBrightonBard.

I look forward to interacting with you there. Cheers.

FINAL THOUGHTS

When I had the idea of this book, my goal was to create an enjoyable time capsule of memories that Albion fans could enjoy for decades. I hope that's what you feel I've delivered and that dipping into it now and again helps take you back to this most fantastic of seasons.

Four years ago, little could I have known that the desire to stay connected with the club would lead me on this most unexpected of journeys. Appearances on BBC Breakfast, Sky Sports News, and many of the numerous, high-quality Albion-related podcasts were a million miles from my mind back in 2019. It's been a bit surreal at times, but great fun, too.

However, at the heart of this book is a football club called Brighton & Hove Albion, a city called Brighton & Hove, and a county called Sussex, and I'd like to finish by sharing a few (non-rhyming) words that I posted online having just received my Albion+ membership gift in August 2023 in Oklahoma. It best illustrates just how much the club, city and county mean to me and, perhaps, will help you enjoy being an Albion fan even more.

A PAUSE FOR THOUGHT....

Late yesterday afternoon, just as Sussex was heading to bed, a small cardboard package was delivered to me, the contents of which had a far bigger impact on a 51-year-old man from Hove than, logically, it should have.

And I want to try and explain why.

As an ex-season ticket holder, I too have felt the anticipation when piling onto a packed bus at Mill Rd or train at Brighton station.

I too have enjoyed a Piglet's Pantry pie and a beer as chants echo around the Lower West's cavernous concourse.

And, I too have felt the lump in my throat as Sussex by the Sea rings around the Amex as the boys emerge from the tunnel

But now I live 4500 miles away I don't get to, and I miss it more than I can explain.

So, when my Albion+ gift from the club arrived yesterday, I was moved in a way I had not expected.

A little tear, honestly.

They say absence makes the heart grow fonder and, man, do I miss our club, our city and our county.

Tomorrow, no matter where you are, look around and find something you'd miss if you had to leave. The chat with locals down the pub perhaps, that special view that you enjoy from the Downs, or your favourite walk along a local footpath.

Don't get me wrong; if I move back to Sussex one day, I'd miss things from here in Oklahoma too.

It happens wherever we are.

It is inevitable.

But this afternoon, as I type this, it is the togetherness, the identity and the sense of belonging that I'm aware that being a supporter of the Albion gives you and me.

I mean, I've never met you, have I? But here we are, two humans, connected because of our love of the club.

I don't know what's driven me to write all this, but on this Tuesday night in Sussex, let's pause to think about the thousands of people who have helped the Albion in our legendary journey over the last 122 years as we wouldn't be connected without them, and it's through their efforts we get to enjoy this incredible time in our club's history.

It won't be long until you next squeeze on a bus/train. It won't be long until you next enjoy a Piglet's Pantry pie and beer. It won't be long until you feel the lump in your throat as Sussex by the Sea rings around the Amex as the boys emerge from the tunnel.

And when you do, cherish every second.

BRIGHTON & HOVE ALBION

We're Brighton & Hove Albion Football Club,
One of the best run in the land.
And this season, a European tour,
Is a trip that we've got planned.

It will be the first time in our history,
And whilst it promises to be fun.
You'd have been mad if you'd suggested it,
When we were wallowing in League One.

So, keep the faith if you're not a Brighton fan,
And your team aren't doing well.
As in 1997, ours nearly died,
And yet here we are, bloody hell.

I hope our incredible story gives you hope,
It's taken lots of blood and sweat and tears.
As well as plenty of luck, a man called Tony,
And the best part of 30 years.

Milton Keynes UK
Ingram Content Group UK Ltd.
UKHW050805071023
430045UK00003B/41

9781739570101